SKATER GIRL

An Archaeology of the Self

MIROLAND IMPRINT 46

 Canada Council   Conseil des Arts
for the Arts   du Canada

 ONTARIO ARTS COUNCIL
CONSEIL DES ARTS DE L'ONTARIO
an Ontario government agency
un organisme du gouvernement de l'Ontario

Canadä

Guernica Editions Inc. acknowledges the support of the Canada Council
for the Arts and the Ontario Arts Council. The Ontario Arts Council
is an agency of the Government of Ontario.
We acknowledge the financial support of the Government of Canada.

SKATER GIRL

An Archaeology of the Self

Robin Pacific

MiroLand publishers

MIROLAND (GUERNICA)
TORONTO • BUFFALO • LANCASTER (U.K.)
2024

Guernica Founder: Antonio D'Alfonso

General editor: Michael Mirolla
Editor: Sonia di Placido
Cover design: Joss Maclennan
Interior design: David Moratto
Cover photo: Steve Horan Photography

Guernica Editions Inc.
1241 Marble Rock Rd., Gananoque, ON K7G 2V4
2250 Military Road, Tonawanda, N.Y. 14150-6000 U.S.A.
www.guernicaeditions.com

Distributors:
Independent Publishers Group (IPG)
600 North Pulaski Road, Chicago IL 60624
University of Toronto Press Distribution (UTP)
5201 Dufferin Street, Toronto (ON), Canada M3H 5T8

First edition.
Printed in Canada.

Legal Deposit—First Quarter
Library of Congress Catalog Card Number: 2023951661
Library and Archives Canada Cataloguing in Publication
Title: Skater girl : an archaeology of the self / Robin Pacific.
Names: Pacific, Robin C., 1945- author.
Description: Series statement: MiroLand imprint ; 46 | "MiroLand imprint, 46."
Identifiers: Canadiana (print) 20230590543 |
Canadiana (ebook) 2023059073X | ISBN 9781771838634 (softcover) |
ISBN 9781771838641 (EPUB)
Subjects: LCGFT: Essays. | LCGFT: Creative nonfiction.
Classification: LCC PS8631.A235 S53 2024 | DDC C814/.6—dc23

"All through the night till dawn the ship sailed on."
—**Homer,** *The Odyssey.* Book 2, 1. 434.

For my best friend,
Joss Maclennan

And for my brother,
John Bell

CONTENTS

SKATER GIRL

An Archaeology of the Self

ON TRUTH, MEMORY, AND THE NATURE OF THE SELF

"**Nature never set** forth the earth in so rich tapestry as divers poets have done; neither with pleasant rivers, fruitful trees, sweet-smelling flowers, nor whatsoever else may make the too-much-loved earth more lovely; her world is brazen, the poets only deliver a golden."
—Sir Philip Sidney, *The Art of Poesie*

———

"I am the way and the truth and the light. No one comes to the father except through me."
—*The Gospel According to John,* 14:6

———

"What is truth, said jesting Pilate, and did not stay for an answer."
—Opening sentence, Sir Francis Bacon, "On Truth"

———

The gospels are perhaps the first "faked" memoirs. Purporting to be first person accounts, they were written at least thirty-five years after the death of Jesus, because Mark, the first Evangelist, mentions the destruction of the temple by the Romans, which happened in 70 AD.

Also, they are clearly shaped to appear to fulfill the prophesies in the Old Testament Book of Isaiah—elaborate predictions about a humble messiah. So much for "the Gospel truth."

At a dinner party once in Vancouver, my friend Stuart said: "In the Middle Ages, truth was faith; in the Enlightenment, truth was science; in what I'm calling our Age of Authenticity, truth is feelings."

Perhaps no other literary event has evoked as many "feelings," on both sides, as the exposé of James Frey's "memoir" *A Million Little Pieces*. A narrative of addiction, recovery, and redemption, it was first selected by Oprah Winfrey (the reigning goddess of the Age of Authenticity) for her book club, which led in part to sales of five million books and translation into twenty-nine languages. Thesmokinggun.com investigated Frey's claim that he had been in jail and found it to be a fabrication, along with much of the rest of the book.

Originally written as a novel, Frey simply re-categorized his book as a memoir at the suggestion of his publishers. At first Oprah defended Frey, saying that the book had helped many people struggling with addiction. (A young relative of mine, who overcame alcoholism, was inspired by it.) She then changed course, had Frey and his publisher, Nan Talese from Doubleday, on her show again, and forcefully attacked them both for lying.

The publisher offered to refund the cost of the book to anyone who had bought it directly from them, as long as they "felt" that they had been defrauded. The controversy raged on, between those who defended "the truth," such as Maureen Dowd, and those who defended "the feelings."

"'The story' supplants the memories."
—Kim Pittaway, Director of the King's College MFA in
Creative Nonfiction, at a talk in Halifax, August 2019.

While wondering how I would ever find an entry point into the huge area of research about human memory, in neuroscience and other fields, I came across a five-part series on Netflix called *The Mind, Explained*. Like many documentaries about science, the episodes are deceptively simple but actually convey complex information. The first half-hour episode is about memory.

Most people remember vividly where they were and what was happening at a particular moment in history that has an impact on millions of people. The death of Princess Diana, for example, or the bombing of the World Trade Center. Yet even these memories can be deceptive, slippery. One young woman remembered that, when the Twin Towers were attacked, her mother was working in the city, and she could see smoke billowing across Long Island Sound from her elementary school window. In fact, her mother was working in Connecticut; the smoke, forty miles away from her school, was moving in the opposite direction; and her school didn't have windows on the side of the building that faced Long Island Sound.

On average, people misremember about 50% of the details of a recollected episode. A sensory event—playing a musical instrument, for example—is experienced in several parts of the brain, and then coordinated by the hippocampus, the centre of memory. (London cab drivers actually have much larger than average hippocampi.) If the purpose of memory is to record the past, the brain does a very poor job of it. Various activities can improve memory, such as meditation, or as I recently read, drawing something rather than writing it down. Strong emotions, centred next to the hippocampus in the amygdala, form more detailed and accurate memories. So does remembering or visiting a particular place where significant events happened. The best way to improve memory, however, is narrative —constructing and telling a story.

But human memory is still a remarkably flawed endeavour. It's frighteningly easy to implant false memories in subjects, through suggestion, repetition and "confirmation." After two or three interviews, subjects concoct details and entire narratives, and are convinced of their veracity.

What then is the purpose of memory? It seems that the same parts of the brain come into play when we imagine the future—that when we daydream, our consciousness shifts back and forth between remembering the past and imagining the future. It is this interplay, researchers speculate, that creates a sense of self.

Montaigne, the progenitor of the literary essay, believed the purpose of the form is to both create and understand the self.

Thomas Merton, the Trappist monk who was such an influential thinker in the sixties, believed that we all have a true self and a false self. The latter is what we acquire to get along in the world, the face we put on to greet the face of others. (I've always loved this line from one of the Shakespeare sonnets: "They are the lords and owners of their faces.") The true, authentic self is our essence, our unique and special being, loved by God. We can discover, as it were, this true self through prayer and meditation.

Carl Jung also believed in a true and false self. In our young adulthood, our psychic task is to create a healthy ego, a persona we can use to navigate through the tasks of maturity, making a living, forming relationships and so on. In order to come into our true self, which can only happen in middle age, we have to acknowledge and integrate the shadow self, our so-called dark side. Something like the fourth step in twelve-step programs, where addicts are encouraged to make an inventory of their faults and then, in subsequent steps, to make amends to whoever they have harmed. As in Merton, this is a profoundly spiritual idea of the self.

"If you believe in a soul, then you can be one self, but otherwise the self is endlessly malleable."
   —Alena Oosterhuizen, in conversation over dinner at Rasa, Toronto, September 5, 2019.

Ironically, Michel de Montaigne, writing in the 1500s, seems more contemporary than either Merton or Jung in his thinking that the self is not set, not fixed, but mutable. "I grasp it as it is now, at this moment when I am lingering over it. I am not portraying being but becoming."
   —From "On Repenting," in Michael Screech's 1991 translation.

Montaigne may have predicted the Orwellian world of *1984*, when Winston Smith finally states, and believes, that 2+2=5. Or indeed, the strange story of Patty Hearst, the heiress who was kidnapped in 1974 by the Symbionese Liberation Army, allegedly kept for weeks, tied up and blindfolded in a closet, and repeatedly raped. She emerged as a slogan-spouting, gun-toting (and gun-firing) bank robber, for which she was convicted and sent to jail. She then married one of the guards. So who exactly was she? Pretty, pampered granddaughter of William Randolph Hearst, or Tania (the name she took after Che Guevara's Communist companion), the militant revolutionary?

— — — —

Sallie Tisdale, in the fine essay "Chemo World" (from *Violation: Collected Essays*), avers that cancer, or more properly its treatment, strips patients of their very personality. Losing one's hair is the least of it.

> To be sick this way is to have a kind of existential wound. One's life is taken apart like a motor, screws and facings laid along the table until it is just parts and nothing is left whole.
> What makes the self a self? With cancer and its treatments, the aspects of identity erode like sand in a tide, inexorably, constantly. You are a person who does things (work, family, hobby, art, sports), a person who fills roles (plumber, father, singer, tennis player), a person with an interior life unlike any other, and it all disappears. Who are you without these things? Who is the person who can't read a book or tie her shoes, can't make love, cook supper, or follow a conversation—who may never do such things the same way again?

— — — —

If memory and the self are so unreliable, who are we when we write? Who do we write, which self, which (possibly false) memories?

— — — —

New developments in technology are further eroding any sense of a stable self, or perhaps of a self at all. CRISP-R, which stands for Clusters of Regularly Interspaced Short Palindromic Repeats (in DNA), allows practitioners (not all of them doctors, apparently) to edit genes to prevent diseases, and ultimately to create "designer babies"—six feet tall, blonde, blue-eyed geniuses with athletic prowess, presumably. This is not science fiction. According to the documentary *Human Nature*, DNA editing is already being used to prevent some diseases.

There are few or no government guidelines and recommendations, not to mention regulations, and a quick search will turn up numerous companies trying to sell you—what? A Franken-person? We think of our DNA as the bottom line of our identity, the unique seedbed of our selfhood. What will our memories be if our genome is genetically altered? What will be true?

But perhaps it is language which forms our human identity? I know dolphins and trees communicate, but they don't write sonnets or paint the Sistine Chapel. We are meaning-making machines, and it is language that makes meaning. But, here again, the very heart of our selfhood is being challenged by technology. The thesis of Alan Turing's prescient essay "Computing Machinery and Intelligence" is that, as described by Jacob Berkowitz in a 2019 *Globe and Mail* article, "the ultimate test of an intelligent computer would be its ability to communicate in a way indistinguishable from a human." And so we come to ChatGPT and its siblings and offspring, and the firestorm of protests from educators, scientists, artists, and writers. A crisis in higher education. The strikes by WGA writers and SAG-AFTRA actors. Not to mention the widespread existential crisis in society at large. These programs or bots can now use, without permission or fear of copyright infringement, the works of published authors to "learn" how to imitate them. It can generate, as a random example, a poem by Philip Larkin which cannot be distinguished from anything he has written. Who, or what, is Philip Larkin now?

In a 2019 *New Yorker* article amusingly but rather ominously titled "Can a Machine Learn to Write for the New Yorker?", John Seabrook explains: "By attempting a task billions of times, the system makes predictions that can become so accurate it does as well as humans at the same task and sometimes outperforms them, even though the machine is still only guessing." In other words, it works much like a psychic reader does, only using a billion times more data, a billion times faster. At the rate at which computing power is increasing annually, as processors get faster and data gets vaster, in five years the machine will equal the number of neurons and their trillions of connectors in the human brain. "One can imagine a kind of Joycean superauthor, capable of any style, turning out spine-tingling suspense novels, massively researched biographies, and nuanced analyses of the Israeli-Palestinian conflict," Seabrook says. We wouldn't have to beleaguer ourselves with whether our memoirs are factual truth or emotional truth, because we writers would become superannuated—like typesetters, assembly line workers, and strawberry pickers. (Yes, they are using AI to pick strawberries—impressive when you think that each plant is different and each berry on each plant ripens at a different time.) How will it feel, as writers, to be superfluous, not needed?

Millions upon millions of people on the earth today are already living in a state of non-being, although in conditions immeasurably worse than any first world redundant writer would face. Stateless, homeless, without adequate food, hygiene, or shelter. Fleeing wars and extreme weather events, unwelcome at practically every border. The geopolitics of late-stage capitalism deems that profit relies less and less on human muscle, on human bodies.

> Nowadays, the project is to render as many people as superfluous as possible.
>
> The novelty is the production at a massive scale of discounted bodies, a residual humanity that is akin to waste. With our entry into a new climatic regime, this process will only intensify. As the global conditions for the production and reproduction of life on Earth keep changing, population politics at a planetary level will increasingly become synonymous with excess and waste

management. (Achille Mbembe, interview on November 30, 2018, in the Norwegian newspaper *Klassekampen*.)

Who are we humans when we become refuse, garbage, scrap, when our consciousness and inner lives are just grist for the data mill? If our memory is flawed, if our genes, our language, and our working bodies are replaced by machines, why should we write? What can we write?

And yet.

I met Diana Meredith on Facebook. I kept seeing her crop up in my feed and reading accounts of her cancer illness. Although the name was vaguely familiar, I had no idea how I knew her. One day she posted a link to her website, and I discovered that she was an artist, producing very powerful and beautiful self-portraits of her nude body, the drawings covered with words about her experiences of cancer. She created the texts using a pen tool that will scroll words as you draw with it. I wrote to her to tell her how much I liked this work, and by the way, how do I know you? It turned out that she had known me thirty years ago, had been the ex-lover of Lina Chartrand, with whom I was running a theatre company called Pelican Players.

I asked to be put on the list of recipients for her "Cancer Letters," which documented her treatments and her physical and emotional responses to her illness. She had a rare blood cancer, and then breast cancer.

We met for coffee, and immediately fell into a friendship based on mutually nourishing conversations about art, politics, feminism. I complimented her on her writing in the Cancer Letters, and said I thought she could have a second career as a published writer. As a matter of fact, she said, I'm in a writing group that meets every two weeks at my house. My husband Peter runs it. Would you be interested?

Diana was the heart of the group, giving feedback as astute as it was generous. She had a big, open laugh that made you smile. We continued to go to art exhibits together, shared studio visits, coffee, and dinner. Everyone has, consciously or otherwise, one or two people in their mind as they are writing. I told Diana that she had become my muse. It made me so happy to please her with my essays.

About a year after I joined the group, Diana's cancer spread to her brain, and she had a craniotomy. At the first writing group meeting after her operation, she read us a piece about the bizarre effects of brain surgery. Looking pale and a little shaky, her voice was nevertheless firm and steady as she spoke. She would put out the things she needed to make breakfast, and then not be able to figure out what to do with them. She would use the bathroom, and not understand how to open the door and go out. Confused and frightened, she relied on Peter to help her with the simplest tasks.

"Throughout it all," she wrote, "Peter was there, Peter was there, Peter was there. And throughout it all I never felt more like Diana."

This simple statement, more than anything I've read, made me ponder the nature of the self, made me ask questions which perhaps have no answers.

Ten days later she came down with the flu. Her breathing became difficult, and her doctor advised Peter to get her to the emergency ward. Her condition worsened quickly; Peter was told her immune system wasn't strong enough to fight the virus and, within hours, she died.

Like each of us, she was the one and only. She was the one and only Diana Meredith.

"It will take a keen eye and keener taste and the keenest of philosophical minds to rescue his lost beloveds from the ravages of time, and it's his inability to control time externally—to resurrect them—that serves as his inner

enemy. In a great memoir, some aspect of the writer's struggle for self often serves as the book's organizing principle ..."
—Mary Karr, *The Art of Memoir,* writing about Nabokov.

My husband, Terry McAuliffe, was diagnosed with a glioblastoma multiforme in September of 2002. That's a fancy phrase for terminal brain cancer. He was given nine to twelve months.

His treatment began with a craniotomy, and radiation, and a steroid called Decadron. Terry developed the "moon face" of steroid users. Slender his whole life, he gained weight, and would often become very emotional, sometimes embarrassingly sentimental. The day he looked fawningly at me and his daughter, with whom I had never gotten along, and said we were his double goddesses, I had to leave the house and go for a walk.

He changed so much—physically, emotionally, and mentally—I could sometimes hardly recognize him. But if I reduced the Decadron he'd start to mumble incoherently, and once he even fell into a coma. I had to feed him the Decadron crushed in a teaspoon of applesauce to bring him back to consciousness. I had a love-hate relationship with that drug.

Then, almost overnight, his condition changed. He lost all the steroid weight, taking on the skeletal appearance of the typical cancer patient. No appetite, constant fatigue. He was often in pain, not from the cancer (because of the brain/blood barrier, the tumour couldn't be felt), but from tiny spinal fractures caused by my old friend Decadron. We brought in a hospital bed, but eventually the stress of caring for him and my own emotional agony became too much, and I was able to get him a palliative bed at Toronto Grace Hospital.

His neurologist, however, thought that a second craniotomy with a chemo wafer (not covered by health care; cost: $13,000), which they would insert into the tumour site, would give him three more months. The doctor looked at the MRI. I looked at Terry. I knew he wouldn't be able to survive such a surgery, but he wanted it, so we did it. When he came out of the Intensive Care Unit he was too weak to be transferred back to the palliative ward, which had unlimited visiting hours. This was at the height of the SARS epidemic in Toronto, and at Toronto Western he was allowed just one and a half hours a day for visitors, who had to wear masks.

His left side was paralyzed; he couldn't form sentences, and often slipped into unconsciousness. But I would position myself so I could lie my head on his shoulder. I played Vivaldi's guitar concertos, his favourite music. And even when he was in a coma-like state, I could close my eyes and *smell* him. No one else smelled like him; I'm sure I could have recognized him blindfolded. Paralyzed, gaunt as a camp survivor, with little brain function—he was still Terry, Terry and no one but Terry.

The hospital finally broke down and let me stay in the room with him overnight.

Throughout his illness we had grown closer and closer, but in those last few days, as I laid my head on his shoulder, hour by hour, I felt we were fused into one being, travelling together towards his death.

Then one afternoon, he kept going, *tout simplement*, and I was left behind. I was somewhere in the stratosphere, alone, in freefall. I was still tethered to him, but that tether grew ever longer and thinner. As frightening as it was, and as lonely, I still felt connected to him. It was the most real experience I've ever felt—was it true? Could you fact check it?

It took me a very long time to stumble back to earth, step by painful and bumpy step. When I got here I was a different person. Not less of myself, but more of myself.

For the raindrop, joy is in entering the river—
Unbearable pain becomes its own cure.

Travel far enough into sorrow, tears turn to sighing;
Is it not that they've wept themselves clear to the end?

If you want to know the miracle, how wind can polish
   a mirror,
Look: the shining glass grows green in spring.

It's the rose's unfolding, Ghalib, that creates the desire
   to see—
In every color and circumstances, may the eyes be open
   for what comes.
   —Ghalib, from the anthology *The Enlightened Heart*,
   edited by Stephen Mitchell

SKATER GIRL

"Her ankles are very weak," the doctor said, pushing my feet up and down and around in painful circles. I started to cry. "You should put her on ice skates."

I was five, and this was the beginning of my career at the Kerrisdale Skating Arena in the west end of Vancouver. I was given figure skating lessons, which involved skating in two large circles that made a figure eight, first on the outside edge of the skate, then on the inside edge. It was excruciatingly boring.

"You have to do it," my mother said. "It's the only way to learn, and to build up your strength."

"Your mother's right," the teacher said. "You should listen to her."

But I could tell, even at a young age, that this instructor, constantly sipping hot chocolate and blowing on her hands, was just as bored as I was. I wondered if she had been a champion figure skater once, like Barbara Ann Scott. I had a Barbara Ann Scott doll, with little white skates and a royal blue skating costume edged at hem and cuffs with what I suspect was real rabbit fur.

When I was eight, my mother heard about a month-long training program on the east side of Vancouver, at the Hastings Park Arena. The girls in this program were all fierce skaters, and tough players of jacks. I spent every minute I could, when I was off the ice, bouncing a little red ball on the cement floor of the arena, trying but failing to beat some of these east end girls. Most of their mothers sat in the stands, knitting them fetchingly adorable skating skirts that were fluted along the hem, with a contrasting stripe made from angora. To make one involved casting a thousand stitches on circular needles. I begged my mother to knit me one, but she just laughed scornfully and went back to her detective novel. It was clear where my compulsive reading habit had come from. "Eyes off the printed word!" was my father's frequent demand. "Go outside and play!"

To be fair, my mother did create terrific skating outfits for me. She cut down my older sister's outgrown tartan skirts and bought me matching sweaters and bonnets, and even knitted knickers. Once for Christmas she gave me a pale blue tartan skirt, with hat, bonnet, and knickers in what was called "powder blue." But I still felt like a second-class citizen without one of those little flute-y flirty knitted skirts.

One day a skater turned up who outshone everyone else. She was the star skater in that club, still only twelve years old. I watched her wizardry in awe. All the other girls spoke about her in whispery voices. Most wondrous of all, she had a different-coloured knitted skating skirt for every day of the week. She was late to the program because the week before she'd had a serious fall and couldn't skate for ten days. We didn't know the word "concussion" then.

With two hours of lessons, practice, and free skate every morning, I couldn't help but become a better skater. By the end of the month, I could do a simple jump, a spiral, a spin and my favourite, something known as the spreadeagle.

When I returned to the Kerrisdale Arena, I was surprised, first, that no-one in Kerrisdale played jacks, and second, that I had become a skating star. (Exactly two months later, jacks became a fad in Kerrisdale—how did memes work back then?) And I was really fast. Faster than anybody except my best friend Philip, known to my family as Flippy, who could just keep up with me.

"C'mon Flippy," I'd shout. "Race me!" And we were off, tearing around the rink, skating as fast as we could, then swooshing up to a dramatic stop on one skate. That feeling of freedom, of no limits, of flying across the ice.

Other children had to get out of our way or risk being knocked over. Some began to be afraid of us, and we started teasing them. At first in fun, then it got meaner. One girl had a hat with a very long tail, with a pompom on the end of it. We'd swoop by her and wind the tail around her neck, to her fury and our delight. "Leave me alone," she cried, helplessly. I was mortified when I was given an identical hat for Christmas that year. "Why won't you wear it?" my mother said. "It's so cute."

Soon we were chasing children, even ones who were bigger than us but not as fast. They would skate off the ice, or crash into the boards to avoid us: the eight-year-old ice-skating avengers from hell. "Give us your snack money and we won't chase you," we said. Then it became: "Give us your snack money or we'll slam you against the boards. Give it to us or we'll beat you up." We were running an extortion racket, right there in the mid-1950s in an upper middle-class neighbourhood in what was at the time a backwater provincial town. At the end of the sessions, we feasted on hot dogs, ice cream bars, and cup after cup of hot chocolate, bought with our stolen money.

It was heaven. The feeling of absolute power, absolute control, was absolutely intoxicating. Knowing I could bend others to my will, make them do my bidding, was a state of no limits, no edges. No shame, no remorse, only the beauty of speed and the sweet power of instilling fear, of being faster and stronger than everyone else. I loved being a bully.

I came home from school one day to find my mother white of face and thin of lip. "Come into the back room," she said, "right this minute."

This little room behind the kitchen was where she kept her sewing machine and ironing board and was used only for dressmaking and dressing downs. A summons to the back room was very serious indeed. She was shaking.

"I got a call from the skating club this morning. Read this," she said, and handed me my membership card. "What does it say? Read it. Out loud."

"It says Robin Bell is a member in good standing of the Kerrisdale Arena Figure Skating Club."

"In good standing. Tell me, what does that mean? What does that mean, in good standing? *In good standing?*" My mother had a habit of repeating herself.

"Good behaviour?"

"That's right, it means respect. It means being nice to other children. It means playing by the rules. You've made me ashamed of you, Robin, really ashamed! You've been suspended from the Club. I'm absolutely mortified!"

The lecture continued, but I'd stopped listening. I was indeed suspended from the Club for the rest of the season and forbidden to play with Flippy for a month. We were pariahs at school. My figure skating career was over.

I still skated, up into my forties when arthritis made it too painful. I still enjoyed the feeling of skimming over the ice, of a certain freedom, but the ecstasy I'd felt in my bullying days was gone. I did, after all, come of age in the 1950s, when smart girls like me were told not to take up too much space, not to ask too many questions, not to give too many right answers. The feeling of no boundaries became its opposite. Life was nothing but boundaries, edges, and limits. Indeed, nothing but shame and remorse.

But some part of me had tasted a strange form of immortality, of liberation from the ethical ties that keep society safe. To this day I think I understand how a dictator feels, even what it would feel like to torture someone. The one who tortures plays God, has the power to hurt or not hurt, to kill or let live. Slamming a kid, a kid bigger than me, against the hoardings of the skating rink gave me that feeling of liberating, God-like power.

"Nothing human is alien to me," as the saying has it. We all have a coward and a bully inside us, we all grovel in fear, and we all raise the whip. Children, of course, cry in terror if they are the victim, and crack that whip if they are the terrorist bully. But we adults have the power, as the case may be, to stand up and face our tormentor, or to lower that arm and drop the weapon.

It's just not as much fun. Not nearly as much fun as flying across the ice—fearless, invincible, and cruel.

UP ON CYPRESS STREET

From the age of three—the age at which in the 1950s children could wander outside freely—the block of Cypress Street between 52nd Ave. and 54th Ave., in the middle-class suburb of Kerrisdale, was my world. I learned taxonomy from knowing every house, who lived in each one, and whether they had children my age. The Wahldorfs lived two doors north of us; the Sedgewicks, our immediate neighbours, had older daughters who were either married, or working as secretaries while waiting to get married, so they were of little interest. On the other side, just south of us, lived the Millhouses, with daughter Judy, and son Tommy, who was a little dull and phlegmatic but part of our group nonetheless. Ann Robertson was across the street, and Libby Hornswell lived across the street and a few houses south. The Blankenberms occupied the northeast corner house.

My earliest memory is being pulled in a red wagon by my older brother and sister, accompanied by all the Cypress Street children, down to the Milky Way on 57th Avenue to buy Dubble Bubble gum. The advent of Dubble Bubble was a momentous event—it had just come on the market. How did we all know about it? This was before we even had television. Perhaps it was advertised on the radio; perhaps the Milky Way promoted the launch date.

"Faster," my sister cried to my brother who was pulling the wagon. "Go faster!"

"Yeah," Tommy Millhouse said. "I wanna taste that gum."

"And blow bubbles," Diana Wahldorf said. "Can't wait to blow bubbles!"

"I've got my two cents," Beady Blankenberm said. "I'm all set."

This is possibly my first venture off the block. My brother opens up the gum and shows me the comic, with its waxy surface, its light dusting of sugary pink powder from the gum. He reads it to me, and I laugh, even though I don't understand the joke. I stuff the gum in my mouth. It's huge, I'm drooling because it takes up so much space I can barely manage to chew it. I can still taste that delicious, chalky, fat sweetness. That sense of fullness.

Bored one afternoon, I wander into the Wahldorfs' backyard to play on their swing set. Diana Wahldorf hangs upside down by her knees from the top cross bar, her bright red shorts vivid against the blue summer sky. Mrs. Wahldorf sits in a chair, watching her. I am maybe seven; Diana a year or two older. Her screams of rage and fear shred the air.

"Please get me down," she shrieks. As she writhes and wiggles, her upside down ponytail bounces up and down and sideways. Mrs. Wahldorf always pulled Diana's hair back so tight it must have scraped her scalp. "Please, please help me mummy, please! I can't get down, my legs hurt so much! Mummy, I'm going to die! Help me!" Her screams are so loud Mrs. Wahldorf has to lean in toward me to say, in a calm and reasonable voice: "I'm teaching Diana an important lesson about life. She has to learn that she must get herself out of whatever she gets herself into."

"But the bar is hurting her, and she's scared." Mrs. Wahldorf's eerie calm chilled me.

"She must learn this important truth. Who will teach her if I don't?"

Diana is sobbing and whimpering by now. Her ponytail has stopped bouncing, but her red shorts still shine bright against the sky.

I turn and run home as fast as I can.

I guess Diana did, somehow or other, manage to get herself down from that cross bar. I'm not sure the lesson she learned from this was the one her mother intended. All I remember is the sound of her anguished cries for help, my own terror.

Mrs. Wahldorf was originally from Greece, and she never missed an opportunity to tell us children that Greece was the birthplace of democracy, and that the culture of Greece was infinitely superior to this little primitive town of Vancouver. God knows she was right, but even as children we felt patronized and insulted.

Diana was the eldest of three. Next to her in age was Larry, who was a little pudgy and who was called Lardo by the whole school, with the casual cruelty of the times. Sybil was the youngest. She too had a ponytail pulled taut. She had a habit of moving her head from side to side when she talked, her thick straight hair also swinging from side to side for emphasis. She wore glasses which gave her a serious demeanour and made her seem far older than her age. When she was six, Sybil Wahldorf accepted Jesus Christ as her personal saviour, and enjoyed coming over to our house to try to convert us. My parents were greatly amused by this. They were especially delighted by her enthusiastic hymn singing.

"Sing us the one about building your house upon a rock, Sybil, it's our favourite."

Sybil complied, belting the song out in her throaty lounge singer voice:

> The wise man built his house upon a rock
> The wise man built his house upon a rock
> The wise man built his house upon a rock
> And the rains came tumbling down.

This was accompanied by hand gestures—one fist bumping the other for the rock, fingers miming the rain—which she generously taught us, and in which we happily joined:

The rains came down and the floods came up
(hands down for the rain, up for the flood)
The rains came down and the floods came up
The rains came down and the floods came up
And the house on the rock stood firm
(fist on fist again).

My mother and father, and older sister and brother, roared with laughter, which did nothing to discourage Sybil from singing *It's in the B-I-B-L-E, that's the book for me*, in her deep baritone, and telling us we should welcome Jesus into our cold, hard hearts.

I once offered to give her 50 cents, my entire allowance, if she would stand in the middle of the road and shout out the swear words I whispered in her ear. We got through damn, ass, and shit, but she balked at fuck. Being a principled little child, she wouldn't accept payment, as she rightly didn't feel she had fulfilled her side of the bargain.

Mrs. Wahldorf was fond of phoning my mother to complain about us, especially my older brother, who embodied the concept of mischief, and who had managed to connect a baseball with one of the Wahldorf's basement windows, or had run their sprinkler for hours when they were away for the day.

"This would never happen in Greece, the birthplace of democracy, where children know their place, and you must properly punish that boy for his own good. You should make him save up his allowance, and pay for that window. Not to mention what our water bill will be this month, after the sprinkler running the whole entire day! This is unacceptable. In my country, Greece, we would never allow something like this to happen."

At the dinner table, my mother told us with great relish how she would put down the phone, continue making dinner, and pick it up every five minutes or so, "Yes Mrs. Wahldorf, you're absolutely right, I'll be sure to discipline him."

How we laughed, how effortlessly we scapegoated that whole family.

Beady Blankenberm, so called because she had small, beady eyes, was the youngest of four girls. Her older sisters all sewed their own clothes on the dining room table. Mr. Blankenberm came home for lunch every weekday, so the dresses-in-making, the sewing machine, the ironing board, and all the sewing paraphernalia were swept away to make room for a white linen tablecloth (washed and ironed by Mrs. Blankenberm or one of the three older daughters), white linen napkins, the good silver, and the good china. After lunch this would all also be taken away, and sewing would recommence. Why don't they just eat lunch at the kitchen table like we do, I thought, and save all the good linen, silver, and china for Sunday dinner?

They were all great cooks and bakers, the Blankenberm girls, and it was Beady who taught me how to make cupcakes. Like Sybil Wahldorf, she felt a need to take over my religious education. My assimilated Jewish father and my lapsed Catholic mother were great skeptics and atheists, which troubled Beady's little Anglican heart. She dragged me to a church group for girls called Explorers, which met at St. Mary's Anglican Church on 37th and Larch. We had to wear middies, which were vaguely like sailor suit tops, and berets. At one meeting it was announced that there was to be an Explorer rally—a jamboree!—in New Westminster. Notices were sent home. Every girl must have an ironed middy and wear her hat. There were 300 girls in that rally, 299 of whom remembered to bring their beret.

The Explorers decided to have a bake sale and contest for Christmas, and we were all instructed to bake a cake. The only rule was that it had to be made from scratch. Since my last name was Bell, I decided I would make a cake in the shape of a bell, perfect for Christmas. I was on fire with this vision. I rushed home from school and baked my cake, from scratch, and then began to cut it into the shape of a bell. One side looked different, so I cut it again. And then that side didn't look right. And then there was just this skinny cake that looked like nothing at all. I was desolate—we had to be there with our cake at five o'clock. I had let down the side, and Beady's frowning face would be there to remind me.

My mother, who for once had some clue about what was going on with me, was actually very nice and helpful, which is perhaps one reason I remember this story so clearly.

"Take this," she said, handing me a few dollar bills.

"Run down to the store and get a cake mix and buy one of those cans of prepared icing. No one will ever know the difference."

The square cake was baked, on time, and I iced it and decorated it with a Christmas tree. The boughs were made out of sparkly green sugar, the trunk was chocolate sprinkles, and the decorations were tiny red gumdrops. I skulked off to St. Mary's, put the cake in the back row, and sat down beside Beady. The cakes were lined up on benches that had been dragged up in front of the altar. We children and our parents sat in the pews. My mother was not in attendance. She scorned any event for children, as well as any kaffee klatches with other housewives, preferring to stay home reading, and smoking one Du Maurier cigarette after another.

To my great consternation, my cake won first prize, and was auctioned off at the highest bid. And, of course, Mrs. Blankenberm bought it. Every day that week Beady brought a slice of it in her lunch. "Mmm, this cake is so good," she would say, looking at me suspiciously with her beady eyes. Did she know I hadn't baked it from scratch? I never asked, and she never told.

A number of important things happened when I was in Grade Three. A new teacher named Rhonda Penner came to our school. In retrospect I think she was one of those few adults at the time who actually liked children and, for that Mad Men era, she was very enlightened. The Province of British Columbia, in some kind of bizarre insistence on uniformity, sent out an edict that all left-handed children would have to write with their right hand. Miss Penner moved my desk beside Philip Clairmont, the only other left-handed child in the class. We struggled and struggled to write and do arithmetic. We were both at the top of the class, but now we were falling behind rapidly. After a few weeks Miss Penner declared the undertaking to be ridiculous and inhumane, and allowed us to write with our left hands again.

Out of this grew one of the great friendships of my life. Philip Clairmont, who my family called Flippy, and I became close allies with secret codes, behaviours, and passwords. Not to mention our career in crime at the Kerrisdale Arena. He was allowed to take the tram up West Boulevard to the village of Kerrisdale by himself. After a long and determined campaign of alternately begging and sulking, I was given permission to go with him. What hitherto unexperienced freedom! With a quarter each in our pockets for treats, and a nickel for tram fare, we ruled the world. How thrilled and grown up I felt, climbing up into the tram, handing my nickel to the driver, watching the familiar stores rush by the window. I wonder if my mother felt her heart give a little at the sight of me; if she knew, as I did in some subtle but sure way, that even as a child, I was leaving home.

Flippy's parents had a cottage at Boundary Bay, and that summer between Grade Three and Grade Four, I was invited to spend a week there. I was blissfully happy; I had been bored and lonely all summer while Flippy was away. His parents, having raised Flippy's two older brothers, had pretty much given up on childrearing and left Flippy to his own devices.

We made up more games. Flippy was the instigator; as a boy he had more courage, was used to thinking up independent ventures. But I was a more than willing participant, and soon enough came up with ideas for mischief of my own. We found bulrushes and dipped them in kerosene and lit them with matches stolen from his kitchen. At night we wandered the streets of the little cottage community with our fiery torches lifted high, singing *Alouette, gentille alouette*, over and over. We never tired of shouting out this song, arms wrapped around each other's waists, torches blazing. Did other cottagers complain about the noise, worry about our safety, about a fire hazard in a dry August week? If so, we never knew about it.

Another one of our rituals involved finding obscure places where we could pee, in daylight, without getting caught. The places we chose were designated as Public Peeing Place #1, #2 and so on. "Race you to Public Peeing Place #3," one of us would shout, and off we'd go.

"Last one there's a dirty rotten egg!" We had to be quick, and get our shorts down, our peeing done, and our shorts back up in record time. The only one I remember clearly was peeing in someone's kindling box on their front porch. The box had a heavy lid, which we'd lift up for each other, so we could climb in by turns to pee. It involved quite a lot of derring-do, and Flippy had the clear advantage.

But our main daytime activity consisted of the equally serious crime of stealing chocolate bars. Because Boundary Bay is just over the U.S. border, Maple's Variety Store carried such hitherto unknown pleasures as All Day Suckers, Crunch, Snickers and Tootsie Rolls, not available in Canada. We prepared carefully for our miscreant excursions, dressing in shorts with elastic waists and T-shirts long enough to pull over the waistband of the shorts. We had a nickel each to buy something, wrangled from Flippy's unsuspecting mother.

Philip went to the cash register and paid for a chocolate bar, chatting with the kindly old man who owned Maple's Variety Store.

"Beautiful day, isn't it? Looks like we'll be going for a swim this afternoon. And maybe for a car ride after supper. My mum's making meatloaf tonight."

"Sounds good," the old man said. "Be careful you watch those tides. Child got caught in the incoming tide once."

Meanwhile I was busily stuffing candy in the waistband of my shorts, pulling the T-shirt down to hide the bulges. Then it was my turn to buy a chocolate bar.

"I'll take a Dixie cup please," I said. "Or maybe a vanilla cone. Gee, I can't decide ..."

We burst out of the store, Flippy laughing loudly.

"Flippy," I said sternly, "bite your cheeks. You can't let him see us laughing."

Philip started to run. "Stop!" I yelled. "That looks even more suspicious. We have to walk slowly." So we bit the inside of our cheeks, and insofar as eight-year-olds can saunter, we sauntered nonchalantly across the road, back to the cottage and into our room, calling out, "Hi Mum, Hi Mrs. C." as we quickly walked past the kitchen.

The room was small and dingy; it might once have been painted white. It contained one bunk bed and a small dresser for Philip's clothes. I kept mine in my suitcase under the bed. As the guest, I'd been allowed to choose upper or lower bunk; naturally I chose the top.

"Report to the upper deck," I said. "Show me watcha got!"

We faced each other sitting cross legged on my bed, and pulled out our pelf. I produced two Tootsie Rolls, three Tootsie Pops, a Crunch, candy cigarettes and two Snickers. Philip had an All Day Sucker, two licorice pipes with red candy sprinkles to look like the end was burning, and a "diamond ring"—a huge zircon-like hard candy shaped like a diamond, on a looped string, which you wore on your finger and sucked until you got to the chocolate at its heart. We pretended to smoke the cigarettes and the cigars.

"Flippy, I have to pee now," I said.

"Me too."

And off we went, to deposit some uric acid on some unsuspecting neighbour's kindling.

They say there's a God that watches over drunks, idiots, and children.

The week was over too soon. Just as I was drifting off to sleep on our last night, I suddenly jerked awake with one of those upsurges of anxiety upon falling asleep that would become so familiar in later life.

"Flippy," I said, "we are going to be stopped and searched at the border, and when they find all this candy they will know we stole it. We could get arrested, we could go to jail. We have to eat it all now, right now. All of it. Now!"

So Flippy climbed up on my top bunk and we started to eat and eat and eat. Suddenly the door flung open and there stood Mrs. C., who until that moment had more or less ignored our existence. I was shaking with fear—this was it, we were caught, she would tell my parents, they'd never let me play with Flippy again, we'd face jail time.

"You children!" she shouted, as we cowered on my bunk. "Eating candy AFTER brushing your teeth. Get out of bed this instant and brush your teeth again!"

So, my life as a criminal went unpunished. When we went back to school in the fall, we became obsessed with skipping, which was something only girls did. But Flippy and I skipped together.

"Sissy!" some of the girls shouted at him. "Mama's boy! Why don't you go play with the other boys?" We both ignored this, working on our jumps and turns:

> On the mountain stands a lady
> Who she is I do not know
> All she wants is gold and silver
> All she wants is a fine young man.
> So come in dear Flippy, while I go out to play.

I had to run out, and Flippy had to run in, without tripping or even touching each other or, of course, the rope. We perfected this and many other manoeuvres.

One day the principal, who was actually named Cecil Hardwick, called Flippy into his office—something in itself to occasion great awe and terror.

"Young man," Philip reported him saying, "you have to stop playing skip with the girls. Do you want to grow up funny? Do you want to become a sissy? You don't want to be a sissy, now do you? Skipping is not a manly activity. Do you want me to call your mother?"

Flippy, who had been the fearless collaborator, and often the instigator, in many of our adventures and pranks, capitulated to authority immediately and stopped playing skip with me. I felt an acid contempt for his cowardice, and to this day I harbor a certain lack of respect for him. I felt it was a sign of a weak character. It was the beginning of the end. We continued to be friends for a while, and I initiated many sessions of playing dirty doctor in his garage. "Show me yours and I'll show you mine," was pretty much the extent of it. But one of his older brothers found us with our pants down, told his parents, and Flippy wasn't allowed to play with me anymore.

Our next-door neighbours, the Sedgewicks, were notable for only two things. First, on Hallowe'en, they gave us Pontefract cakes, which, as they proudly told us, came all the way from England. Why they thought children would like those hard and bitter licorice candies, which weren't cakes at all, I do not know. In the little bag of Pontefract cakes were two shiny pennies. At least we could buy some penny candy. The Pontefract cakes mouldered in the bottom of our treat bags, along with the equally loathed Candy Kisses.

One day the news ran up and down the street like an electric current—the Sedgewicks were taking in a boarder, and that boarder was none other than Miss Rhonda Penner, my teacher who I loved with a pure and tender flame. I was thrilled and a little breathless. I happened to have a new pair of red pedal pushers, as we called them then, and I sashayed up and down the street all afternoon, hoping to see Miss Penner move in. I knew that I looked so adorable in those pedal pushers that if she saw me she would fall in love with me, too.

I never did see Miss Penner move in, but that afternoon I achieved something I have never experienced before or since. I was cute. Very cute. Like my friend, Ann, who lived across the street, and whom my family never referred to as other than "Little Annie Robertson". "Would you like to stay for dinner, Little Annie Robertson?" my mother would ask. "Go play with Little Annie Robertson," my sister would advise when I complained of boredom. L.A.R. was genuinely adorable. First, she had the most enviable quality of being petite, a fact that occasionally filled me with inchoate rage. And she actually had a little halo of silky golden curls. Oh, she was cute all right, but that afternoon, in my red pedal pushers, I had something Little Annie Robertson never would: I was *sassy*.

I never lost the thrill of Miss Penner being my next door neighbour and loved to brag about it at school. I don't remember what happened to her. I assume she married and left teaching. I don't know if married women were barred from teaching at that time, but I don't remember any female teacher being called anything other than "Miss".

———

Another news bulletin travelled up and down Cypress Street—the house for sale, across the street and next door to Little Annie Robertson, had been bought by a family from Hong Kong. Rumours spread like poison ivy: the father wasn't coming, he was married to someone else in China, he was sending his concubine with her two children. Our next-door neighbour to the south of us, the father of my friend Tommy Millhouse, was in high dudgeon. He got up a petition and asked everyone on the street, except the Mandelmans, presumably because they were the only Jewish family, to protest the sale of the house. My father, also Jewish, *was* approached for a signature, but he angrily told Dr. Millhouse to leave.

Whether the good Doctor had any legitimate or illegitimate grounds to do this I don't know. I do know that before Diefenbaker brought down the Bill of Rights in 1960, it was entirely legal to have a codicil on the deed of your house saying it could never be sold to Jews, Blacks or Chinese. I believe Indigenous people were not even allowed to own property. My father later told me that, when they were looking at a house to buy after the war, when my mother was pregnant with me, a real estate agent pulled him aside, saying: "Don't worry, this house can't be sold to Jews."

In any case, the Millhouse petition didn't succeed, and one day we saw the moving van drive up. Shortly after, the woman of the house, Mrs. Wong—and it turned out that it was a traditional nuclear family just like every other family on Cypress Street—astonished the neighbourhood by inviting everyone to a cocktail party.

A cocktail party was definitely a cut above the bake sales and kaffee klatches favoured by the other housewives on the block (except for my mother). This was a whole new degree of sophistication, and every one of the adults on the street intended to go to that cocktail party. Even Mrs. Millhouse. Shortly before the appointed hour she bustled through the side door to our kitchen and sat down at our yellow Arborite kitchen table. She was wearing what was called a "sheath," a tight-fitting dress with three-quarter-length sleeves, the hem just skimming her knees, in a pastel brocade pattern that looked like an old piece of drapery. It seemed at least two sizes too small for her. My mother, on the other hand, looked rather elegant in a black cocktail dress with a square cut neckline and long sleeves with black satin cuffs. I thought she looked like a movie star. They both walked awkwardly on their unfamiliar high heels.

"Pour me a drink Dorothy, and make it a stiff one," Mrs. Millhouse said. "I don't drink, I never drink, but right now if I am going to go to this party, and meet those people, I am in need of a very stiff drink!"

My mother, well into her daily ration of several stiff rye and ginger ales, happily complied. Watching avidly from our front porch, I saw Mrs. Wong, dressed in an elegant silk cheongsam, welcome everyone warmly, with charm and grace.

"Wasn't she lovely," I overheard my father saying when they came home. I was sitting on the stairs in the dark.

"I think they'll be a great addition to the neighbourhood," he said. "Their three boys seem very polite and serious. Mr. Wong is clearly a successful businessman. We had quite an interesting conversation about the stock market."

"Oh yes," my mother said. "It was a great party, and it certainly made that old witch Mrs. Millhouse keep her mouth shut for once."

The Wongs were set for life after that cocktail party, and their youngest son became one of our gang.

— — — —

Tired of whatever version of street baseball we were playing, we children gathered on my front porch on summer evenings, night after night, as dusk came so slowly and so gently, and then it was

31

dark, and someone's mother called, and it was time. Sitting on the front porch I kept glancing next door to the Sedgewicks', hoping to catch a glimpse of my beloved Rhonda Penner going out or coming in. Occasionally I saw her with a young man, a man for whom I nurtured a bitter little stone of jealousy. My intense joy at seeing *her* was matched exactly by the misery of seeing *him*.

Once in a while Beady's next-oldest sister Frannie would grace us with her august twelve-year-old presence. What did we talk about, all those hours? We gossiped and argued, but mostly we focused on our communal obsessions: where do babies come from, and what exactly did petting mean? In these matters Libby Hornswell was by far the acknowledged expert. Her mother, who rivaled mine in the number of drinks she could sock back while doing the ironing, tending to the garden, and cooking supper, would answer absolutely any questions, straight up. So, we relayed our wonderings through Libby to Mrs. Hornswell, and Libby would come back to tell us in hushed and conspiratorial tones things we didn't even know we didn't know.

"Come here," Libby said, hissing at me. "I have a big secret. No, come further so no one can hear. You have to promise you won't tell a living soul."

Finally, after many swears and an agreement to buy her a fudgsicle and a Crispy Crunch, she lowered her head and whispered in reverent tones, "Frannie Blankenberm M's!" I must say I give Beady credit for never revealing this most fascinating news about her older sister. All too soon we would all be menstruating, except, of course, for Tommy Millhouse and Lardo Wahldorf—Diana first, then Beady, Libby, me, even, eventually, the adorable Little Annie Robertson.

I wasn't sure if it was an end, or a beginning.

WHITE KITTY

White Kitty's origin story is rather complex. First there was Inkster, obviously a black cat, acquired in 1995. At that time, I was living with my partner Terry, my daughter, and her best friend Christy, who needed refuge from an abusive household. Christy's mom found Inkster in the crosswalk at Bathurst and Wilson in North Toronto and gave him to Christy. Thinking he might be lonesome, we acquired Mango, obviously an orange cat, from a farm near Goderich. All was peaceable in the realm, except for Inkster's occasional forays into the ravine behind our house, whence he would return with disgusting, suppurating wounds that needed treatment at the vet. Then Mango was hit by a car and killed. Some who knew us were sympathetic, others judged us harshly for letting him go outside.

I had a storefront studio on Oakwood Avenue, and one day, looking out the back window, I saw an adorable little orange kitten—the perfect substitute for Mango! I scooped him up and had him neutered and treated for fleas. I named him Dové. By this time the two girls had moved out and we were renting the third floor to a woman from Eritrea, also escaping an abusive household, and her seven-year-old daughter, Clara. Clara adored Dové, but, at five months, he developed kidney disease and died. She was inconsolable. I promised Clara I would get another cat.

In the fall of 2002, Terry was diagnosed with terminal brain cancer and given less than a year to live. But a promise is a promise, and I duly went out to the Etobicoke Humane Society to look for a kitten for Clara. There were two sisters, one grey and one white, about six months old, and since we still had the all-black Inkster, I figured we could get the grey scale in cats. I called Terry, who encouraged me to bring both of them home.

The grey kitten, whom we called Smoke, decamped to a space in the drywall in the basement and never came out. Occasionally Terry, up late at night, would see her streak up the stairs to the food bowl, grab a quick snack, and streak back down—hence the name, Smoke. I eventually trapped her with cat food (recommendations of popcorn and sardines having failed) and put her in the downstairs bathroom. There she stayed, night and day, on a window shelf. I called someone at the Annex Cat Rescue Society, not knowing what to do. Oh, she said, just go down about twenty minutes out of every hour and socialize her. But I'm working at home, I said, I can't do that! Oh, I understand completely. I work also, so I just go down every evening for three or four hours to interact with the cat in MY basement. I'm sure there are some sane people at the Annex Cat Rescue Society, but I wasn't talking with one of them.

In the end, my best friend Joss took me in hand. "Look," she said, "Terry is not well and needs your care and attention. Get rid of that goddamned cat." So I did, and then we were left with Inkster and Smoke's all-white sister. No one could agree on a name for her. Clara called her Paige; her friend called her Snowball; someone else called her Marshmallow, a name more suited to her sweet but passive nature. But none of them stuck.

Now, Inkster was more than a cool cat, he was a great cat. He was smart and I swear he had a sense of humour. He was the master of the side-eye, or of what is known as the gimlet eye, looking down his nose with distaste if he didn't like his food or deemed it insufficient. The white cat, on the other hand, was so bland she didn't even merit a name. So she just defaulted to White Kitty. Joss always said she thought that cat had had a personality transplant. But she became a fixture, never having enough curiosity to want to go outside, thus helping me avoid the great debate.

When Terry died, Inkster went to ground, showing up only to eat. I basically didn't see him for three months. When he re-surfaced he had clearly aged, growing a few white whiskers. Feeling the need for new life in the house, I acquired a barn cat, a tabby, who I named Buxtehude, after the seventeenth-century Danish baroque organ composer. Just because I loved saying that word out loud: Buxtehude, Buxte for short. After Inkster met his maker in 2010, Buxte and White Kitty duked it out for alpha cat, and amazingly, White Kitty came out on top, even though she had by now acquired impressive girth. However, this did not make her any more interesting. During the years we had in Toronto a loathsome crack-smoking mayor, my new partner Frank called her Ford, because she was so white and so fat.

What White Kitty lacked in character she made up in punitive damages. She clawed all the upholstery, which had to be replaced with microfibre animal-proof slipcovers at a cost of thousands. Periodically, and then consistently, for about a six-month period, she decided not to use the litter box. Cleaning bills for carpets were added to her expense account. Joss has never forgotten the day White Kitty looked her straight in the eye and took a dump on the living room rug. The good rug. At one point it got so bad I decided to get rid of her. I advertised her on Kijiji—not a single taker. I called the Humane Society and was sternly and sanctimoniously told that I had taken on this animal for life, for better or worse. You try living in a house full of cat shit and cat piss, was my rude response before I hung up. Finally I called the vet and said I wanted to euthanize her. Well, she said, I hate to put down a healthy animal. Let's try a few things first. Get an extra litter box, empty it every day and see if that helps. Miraculously these measures indeed helped and, except for the occasional out-of-the-box bathroom expedition, White Kitty settled down.

She was always very fearful, hiding out whenever anyone came over, and running like spit for cover whenever the vacuum cleaner made an appearance. Still, her presence in the house became something of a comfort. She and Buxte would sleep on my bed, each one wedged against a thigh, while Mercy the dog slept on my closet floor. I got used to two warm purring bundles on either side of me, Mercy gently snoring in the closet. We were a unit, a unit of four, a household.

But one day White Kitty stopped eating, stopped drinking, stopped using the litter box. I took her to the vet, who did blood work and said she would need an ultrasound to determine if it was thyroid, kidneys, or cancer, and that the treatment would be steroids. I did not want to pay for expensive tests and I had seen what steroids did to Terry. They hydrated her and I took her home, giving her wet food and even baby food. She seemed to grow sweeter and sweeter in her last ten days on this earth. Whenever anyone came over, she would sit purring on their lap, as if she was saying goodbye. I trusted that I would know, and she would know, when her time had come.

So when I woke up one morning and she didn't eat at all, I knew in my bones that this was the end. Still, I went back and forth all day, even calling and making an appointment and then cancelling it. But by the time Frank arrived in the late afternoon, I could see she was fading. I made another appointment, and we wrapped her in the blanket she always sat snoozing on and took her in. We burned a little sage for her. The young vet was amazingly tender and compassionate, checked her over and agreed that her suffering should not be prolonged. She put a catheter in her leg and injected the lethal fluid. White Kitty just slipped away, in my arms, in the most peaceful and beautiful way. I started to cry, and the vet and Frank each put an arm around me. Then all three of us wept.

I miss her. Never again will she wedge her fat body beside me as I sleep, refusing to move when I get up to go to the bathroom. Never again will she sit purring loudly on my lap, depositing vast amounts of impossible-to-remove white fur on my black pants. Never again will she take an occasional dump on Mercy's bed, just for the fun of it. She is gone. Still, I feel the wisp of her little white spirit in the house. A tincture of sweetness in the air.

POSTSCRIPT

There are animals, and then there are pets. Is it right to domesticate an animal solely for our own pleasure, for our needs for companionship? We become so attached to these household gods. I wonder how much I anthropomorphize them, how much I project my own needs, for warmth, for affection. They are dumb witnesses to the events that unfold, the happy and the sad. They are a through-line, a constant in our lives, until they aren't. Mostly they die before we do, and we grieve them like we grieve the loss of people.

In the Great Chain of Being, a notion popular in the Middle Ages and the Renaissance, God is at the top, humans are in the middle, and animals and plants below. But surely the dumb beasts are more evolved than the humans. Exactly which planet are cats and dogs busily destroying? We think of a state of unconditional love as the highest spiritual attainment. Who already got there? Because we have tamed them over the centuries, they depend on us for sustenance. But we depend on them for so much more.

I'm writing this in spring, in Toronto, as we swing into the second year of the global pandemic. Out walking my dog Mercy, now twelve, it seems like everyone got a puppy for Christmas this year. The shelters for both dogs and cats have been emptied out. My dentist tells me she had to drive to Sarnia to get a rescue kitten. I feel it also. Incipient kitten fever. For the first time, I'm considering a designer cat, a Siberian Forest Cat. I know Mercy will be so jealous. I know Buxtehude will once again have to battle for alpha cat. There will be drama. There will be fights. I don't care. I need new life in the house. I crave some excitement in the endless pandemic waste of our days. Yes, another pet. Just the thing.

NOSTALGIA

In my early teens I was sent to an all-girls camp, Camp Kopje, on Lake Okanagan in British Columbia. It was owned by the parents of a school friend, Patsy Broome. On long, lazy summer afternoons, we canoed in groups of three, one in the back who could steer, one in the front who was a strong paddler, and one in the middle for decoration. I sat in the middle.

> *"Hi lo inny minny cah cah m cha cha e wah wah,"* we
>   chanted across the lake to three girls in another canoe.
> *"Heptiminica onica zonica boom ti ally yoo hoo,"* they
>   called back.

These, we were taught, were "Indian" chants. I think many, perhaps most summer camps in that era—the late fifties, early sixties—had an "Indian" ethos. A kind of sentimental, late Romantic, idea of the noble savage, paddling his canoe and running through the woods in buckskins. I could almost catch a fleeting glimpse of this phantasmagoria, looking up from the craft table where I sat making a mosaic tile ashtray for my chain-smoking mother.

> My paddle's keen and bright,
> Flashing like silver,
> Follow the swift goose flight,
> Dip dip and swing.

These were the songs we warbled around the campfire at night. Nostalgia—a longing for a past that never existed. Behind this screen of fake longing for a mythic savage lay the actually savage reality. Real "Indians" were having the Indian ripped out of them, beaten, starved, and sexually abused in residential schools. There were Indigenous children from the Musqueam Reserve at my school in Vancouver, Point Grey Junior High School, but they were invisible to us white students. They could have been ghosts. What must that have felt like for them?

Colonialism is, among other things, the forcible re-naming of one word into another. I remember the shock I felt when I realized for the first time that the words "Douglas" and "fir" were not welded together. That David Douglas did not "discover" this iconic Pacific west coast tree, that it had another name, unknown to me but known to others, somewhere in the vicinity, unseen, unheard—at least by us settlers. (I learn now that one Coast Salish name for the tree, used in the Halkomelem language, is *lá:yelhp*. In the Lushootseed language, the tree is called *čəbidac*.) The chants we so joyfully shouted to each other across the misty lake were a translation of a translation, a simulacrum of language.

A Google search turns up some memories from Doug Broome, Patsy's older brother. The old house, where we ate our meals, was built by a veteran of the Boer War, hence the name Kopje, because the hill behind the house was named Spion Kop, after a Boer War battle site. "The camp carried over the African theme with girls divided into the Watusi, Pygmy and Zulu tribes," Broome states, "and living in cabins called Kaboola, Kabasha and Kaleema." A memory rises up, all of us girls chanting during our after-lunch singalong, "*Kaboola, Kabasha, Kaleema!*" An African theme and an Indian theme.

After the death of the elder Broomes, the house fell into ruin, and was then bought and restored by the region. It now exists as a museum, Gibson House, in Kopje Regional Park.

Broome: "During the restoration of the old house, known to us as Kenya, the skeleton of a young First Nations girl was discovered buried close to the house, and I think of her lying there amused by all the laughter and gambols of her wealthy white sisters, a haunting image of a haunting place."

Blue lake and rocky shore, I will return once more was another song that filled the woodsmoke-scented air in the evenings. I remember well the sweet, pleasant ache of longing the song always gave rise to in me. But longing for what? I was already *actually there*—at the blue lake and rocky shore. Nostalgia not for a past that never was, but for a present I already had.

Six decades later, do I yearn to go back to that lake, that shore? My memories are hardly a haze of romantic canoe trips and camp-fires. I was caught smoking cigarettes, not once, but three times, and in the morning circle one day Mrs. Broome herself came and gave us a special talk about integrity.

"Integrity," she said, looking straight at me. "Do you know what that word means? It's what we expect from all our girls, it's what makes something called character."

I was suddenly hot, and my skin prickled. A current of shame ran through my body. I couldn't look around the circle at the other girls, who I was certain were all looking at me.

I didn't stop smoking, though, and I didn't stop getting caught.

I was addicted, not just to the nicotine, but to the shame. The shame could be counted on to solidify, over and over, the knowledge that I was intrinsically, irrevocably, a bad person. Beyond help or redemption. No amount of what I considered religious claptrap, of repentance and forgiveness and all that nonsense, could penetrate my self-loathing. Only occasionally, swimming in the clear blue lake, in the still calm water, did I find some peace. The weightless-ness of the water seemed to hold me, to buoy me up, and I felt a momentary reprieve.

My nostalgia now is for that fourteen-year-old girl. I would like to go back and tell her that it will take years and years of failing and falling and struggling, but that she will learn, in finally loving others, to let others love her. She will fail and fall and struggle in her work, but gradually succeed, find work she loves, that sometimes matters to other people. She will have great love in her life, and great loss. She will come through the inferno of grief with the last shreds of her self-doubt and shame burned away. With an unshakeable faith in the inherent goodness in the world, and in herself, and in other people. And faith in a just and loving and always present God.

I long for that girl. I long to tell her:

I once was lost, but now am found.
Was blind, but now I see.

I ache as well to reach back in time and make recompense to the Indigenous people we romanticized in the same moment that we ignored their real presence and suffering. Perhaps this is a truer, legitimate nostalgia. I hope I can do better than be a "wealthy white sister" to the spirit of that anonymous girl who died near the old house.

THE HARDEST DECISION
I EVER MADE

The three of us, my parents and I, sat around the yellow Arborite kitchen table, so familiar it was almost invisible. As we were to each other, perhaps.

"Robin, I've enrolled you in Pitman Business School for the summer," my mother said as she cleared the dinner plates. "You need to learn shorthand and typing, so that you'll have something to fall back on if anything ever happens to your future husband. It's at Broadway and Granville, so you can take the bus."

"Listen to your mother," my father said. "Besides, you'll be too bored all summer with nothing to do but get into trouble."

Actually, I was already in trouble, because I was having an affair with Henry, my first lover, whom I had met the year before when I was sixteen. I might have been bored that summer if I hadn't gone to Pitman Business School, but I couldn't have been more bored than I was there, suffering through typing, shorthand, how to write a business letter, simple accounting. Although I admit I did rather enjoy learning shorthand. It was another language, visually beautiful with its swoops and dots. It's rarely used today, except by court reporters and some journalists. It's still much faster to type up shorthand notes than to listen to a long tape and transcribe it.

"All right," the instructor said, "time for a typing speed test. Your grade will be the number of words per minute you type, but all errors will be deducted from your score." We were off, platens clanging as we raced to start a new line. Clickety clackety clickety clackety PING. Soon I was far away from that room, reliving a time in the early spring, when Henry and I made love on Locarno Beach, where the trees gave us a little coverage. The sand was cold on my bare bum, but Henry's kisses were warm and soft. The peaceful sound of the waves coming in, down at the edge of the beach; the smell of the salt in the air. If anyone walked by and saw us, I didn't notice and I didn't care.

"Time's up," the instructor sang out. I had typed on automatic pilot and my speed was excellent. But there were many, many errors, which pulled down my score and sent me near to the bottom of the class. I was mortified because I was used to getting excellent grades in all subjects, but I couldn't pull myself out of the erotic haze, the swoon I swam around in through most of my waking hours.

Henry had gone to work in Nanaimo for the summer, and I was disconsolate. I couldn't seem to find common ground with any of the girls at Pitman Business School, and my other friends were away working at camps, or staying at cottages. I was lonely. One day on my lunch hour he showed up, completely unexpectedly, like a God descending from the aether.

"Come to the Island this weekend," he said. "I can borrow some camping equipment, and the weather will be gorgeous."

This was just pure catnip. Without hesitation, I told my parents that I was going to my friend Judy's family cottage for the weekend. They barely looked up from reading the *Vancouver Sun* (my father) and the *Ladies Home Journal* (my mother). I took the ferry to Nanaimo. Henry had found a spot near a river where we could pitch the tent. That part of the river formed a little shallow pool. We were completely alone. It was a hot summer day, and the water was cold and refreshing. Naked, we stood in the river, about twenty feet apart, and tossed a tennis ball back and forth. Whenever I missed, it splashed in the water, spraying diamond drops of icy water on my sunbaked body. It was late afternoon but the sun was still quite high in the sky. The light glimmered in the leaves of the trees lining the bank, sending dappled shadows across the water. Henry pretended to chase me, and we fell in the water, splashing each other and laughing. Just like Adam and Eve in the garden of Eden, I thought. We made sweet love in the tent that night.

When I got home, my parents were sitting in the living room. "Get in here," my mother said. She looked strangely white and puffy, her eyes swollen. My father was grim-faced, not a hint of the smile in his eyes that I could usually tease out of him, even when being reprimanded for the most serious misdemeanours.

"We called your friend Judy," my mother said, "and her mother said they'd heard nothing of you. I know exactly where you went and what you were doing, you little slut! They don't even have a cottage."

"I'm going to Nanaimo to talk to this man!" my father said.

He came back a day later. "Well," he said, "I met Henry, and we had a good talk. That man's as good looking as a young Adonis. I can understand completely why any seventeen-year-old girl would fall for him. As far as I'm concerned, you can see him, you can sleep with him. I don't think there's anything wrong with it."

My mother's response to this was to rip an electric cord out and throw a precious and valuable lamp with a china base against the side wall of the living room, smashing it to pieces.

"Get out!" she screamed. "Both of you. I never want to see either of you again as long as I live."

So we left. I had nowhere to go, and no money. My father drove me to the YWCA where I could at least get a bed in a room with three other women.

To my surprise, my newly acquired stenographic skills stood me in good stead, and I was able to find a job in an office on Granville Island, with a company that made adding machine rolls. My new boss called my father and asked him why I wasn't in school, where I clearly belonged. My father, liberated at last from his rage-filled and alcohol-fuelled relationship with my mother, bought himself a white Cadillac convertible, and proceeded to have a so-called mid-life crisis, driving around Vancouver with the top down, wining and dining all the women he knew. He came to my office on Granville Island to pick me up for lunch one day, and everyone in the office thought that I had a sugar daddy, or so they let me know, in so many words. He relished telling me about all the women he was seeing, and he continued to encourage me to have sex with Henry, with whom he had formed an odd kind of friendship, partly father and son, partly based on their shared exploits with women. One of whom happened to be his daughter.

My memory of camping by the river that summer weekend became a kind of talisman, something I could hold on to. It was like a white shiny pebble I kept in my pocket, that I could take out and look at whenever I needed solace. I fell asleep at night imagining I was still there, tossing that ball, naked in the river.

By September, when all my friends were either beginning their last year of high school or starting university, I was pregnant.

When I told Henry, he began pacing around his tiny living room in tight, frantic circles.

"What do you expect me to do?" he said. "Jump for joy? You have to get rid of it."

I felt the skin of my face go taut and stiff. I got my coat and let myself out, closing the door carefully and quietly behind me. I walked the six or seven blocks down the hill to Kitsilano Beach and sat on one of the big logs that Vancouver beaches are so known for. It was a golden September evening. There were hardly any people on the beach. The last rays of the sun were warm but my skin was icy. Not just my skin. My very flesh was shivering. I wrapped my cold arms around my cold belly. "I have no choice. I have no choice. I have no choice." The words seemed to speak themselves into my mind as I rocked back and forth on that giant log, back and forth, back and forth.

Henry, who worked on East Hastings, sometimes as a short order cook, sometimes as a butcher's assistant, seemed to know some sketchy people, operating just on this and sometimes on the other side of the law. He knew a woman, he said, who could perform an abortion. He told me it would happen on the following Sunday. But "the woman" got caught and went to jail for two months. The leaves fell, and I was still pregnant. I was starting to show. Eventually she appeared in Henry's apartment. I think I was living there by then. She injected a saline solution into my cervix, gave me some Epsom salts to dissolve and drink, and left. In an hour or so, I started having contractions. I was more than four months pregnant, the age at which they can now keep a foetus alive. In fact, I know a little girl who was born at four-and-a-half months and she's completely normal.

I started to bleed. Henry told me to sit on the toilet. After what felt like hours, but was probably about thirty minutes, I felt a great gush of blood and what seemed like an enormous clot came out of my vagina. Henry flushed the toilet.

The bleeding got worse, and then it got much worse. Henry drove me to the hospital. I was hemorrhaging, the nurse told me. They were able to stop it, give me a D and C—a new phrase that meant Dilation and Curettage, which meant they cleaned the debris out of my uterus.

My family doctor, tall, stern and be-moustached, came to see me in the hospital. He wouldn't look me in the eye. He had a long black coat on, and removed a black hat from over his black hair. He didn't mention what I'd done. He did, however, tell me that there was a new drug on the market which prevented pregnancy. When I got out, he would prescribe it for me.

"Thank you so much." I said. "Please, please, please. Promise me you won't tell my parents?"

"I can't promise you that. You're underage."

To his credit, he didn't tell them, and he did give me a prescription for birth control pills.

I almost died. Many women who had back street abortions did. But some part of me had turned into a hard little ball of sadness, buried deep in my soul. It didn't come to light until many years later when I finally had a child of my own. When my daughter was one year old, I began seeing a therapist, and cried in her office every week for six months. I had flushed my baby down the toilet. I had almost died. Sometimes the grief was so intense I wished that I had.

I never really reconciled with my parents, my mother's drunken rages, my father's prurience.

I was so young, so desperate, and so in love with a man who didn't jump for joy.

POSTSCRIPT

Abortion was legalized in Canada in 1988, when I was forty-three years old.

WATER

I don't want to write tonight. My words are a blocked dam. There is no flow, no energy, there is only resistance. I miss my friend Diana, and I am angry that she is not here, and I am angry that other people are here who are not Diana. My very blood feels stopped. I hate death. I hate death. I hate death. My friend said the other day, first in Bengali, and then in English: "Death comes like a lover with poisoned lips, and he kisses me, and I faint with pleasure." Death comes to me with ice and ashes, and I am faint with disgust. Do not touch me, death, do not assault me, do not think that I desire your appalling sexuality. No flow, only stoppage, blockage, endings. Do not speak to me of transformation when all that goodness and generosity, that searchlight intelligence, is gone, gone for good. Don't pretend that she lives in my heart when all I want is for her, her real physical self, to be here, in this room, to talk to me, to laugh that bright open wild laugh that I miss in some place beyond feeling, beyond prayer, beyond hope. My tears coagulate. My laughter dams up. My mind is a stagnant pond.

MUD

Under the dark brown earth the seeds coil, and I recoil. Do not play me this seasonal hymn of resurrection. Do not speak to me of the light, for when the dark earth begins to move, when the life of the very mud starts to surge up, then I mourn, I mourn, I mourn, for the ones who won't come back each year, the ones who can't come back, try as they might. Try as I might, try and will them into existence, will their physical bodies to be reborn. Memories are not enough, legacies are not enough. I want physicality, life, the symphony of life, the mud. The mud so fertile, so stirring, so alive. The cruel inevitability of this annual renaissance, but the ones I love stay hidden in the brown earth, forever. I want to lie down on the ground and eat the mud. I want to eat death, devour it, once and for all, vanquish it forever.

THE PILGRIM SOUL

The voice of Mr. Sutherland, my high school English teacher (known to all as "Sudsy"), had a peculiar effect on me. As soon as he started to teach, I fell asleep. I didn't nod off, or doze—I put my head down on the desk and fell into a deep, dreamless sleep. This puzzled Sudsy, then annoyed him, and eventually enraged him. He made me stay after school and write out: "I will not fall asleep in Mr. Sutherland's English Class" four hundred times.

One day, I stumbled on a solution. If I held the Grade Twelve textbook under my desk and open on my lap, I could drown out Sudsy's soporific voice, and stay awake. This book was an anthology of classic poetic and prose chestnuts. I read Wordsworth and Coleridge, Keats, Shelley, Byron, Browning and Yeats. Those poets were my first love, as I surreptitiously imbibed some of the best of the canon of English literature while Sudsy droned on in the background.

I was too tall, too gawky, too self-conscious, and too brainy, hopeless at sports. My best friend Vicki was the Canadian Junior Women's Tennis Champion, a title she had held since she was twelve. It was an unlikely friendship, but we bumped along, and spent all our free time together. She could flawlessly imitate every teacher, doing a kind of simultaneous translation sitting beside me, *sotto voce*. I was always being challenged for laughing, threatened with detentions and trips to the principal's office. But every time I heard her speak exactly in the teacher's voice, with just a little time lag, I was convulsed. I didn't care that she never got caught because she was so generous. When we had a field hockey test in phys. ed. she made sure she got to be my partner; then she tapped the ball so gently towards me it was impossible not to hit it. No matter where my returning shot was headed, high, low, left, right—she caught it and sent it back again, right to my feet. I got an A in phys. ed. that year, knowing looks and condescending sneers from the teacher notwithstanding.

In the "play room" in our basement we had a small pool table that my older brother had built in his high school shop class. Every day that school year Vicki and I walked to my house at lunch time, stole cigarettes from my mother, and went downstairs to play pool. We kept track of our games on a little blackboard. The final score: 300–0. From time to time her older brother let her use his car, and on those days we drove to that Vancouver institution known as The White Spot. They slid a tray across the front seats, affixing it to each window, and we scarfed down the best hamburgers I've ever eaten, and still yearn for.

My house, for all its boisterous arguments, door slamming and drinking, was a far more hospitable place than Vicki's. My only memory of her house is going there after school one day, and seeing her mother on all fours in front of the fireplace, trying to find cigarette butts in the ashes. She asked Vicki for her allowance so she could buy smokes, but Vicki had spent it that day at the White Spot. So Vicki often stayed overnight at my house. My sister had married and left home, and we slept in her old room because it had twin beds. And also because Vicki, lithe as an ocelot, could climb out the window onto the garage roof, and from there to the cherry tree to pick cherries for us. I found a copy of *The Catcher in the Rye* among my sister's old books. Hey Vicki, listen to this! We stayed up all night reading it aloud to each other, chapter by chapter.

One day, reading my beloved anthology in Sudsy's class, I discovered (O brave new world. 'Tis new to thee!) Yeats's poem to his lover, Maud Gonne:

When you are old and grey and full of sleep,
And nodding by the fire, take down this book,
And slowly read, and dream of the soft look
Your eyes had once, and of their shadows deep;

How many loved your moments of glad grace,
And loved your beauty with love false or true,
But one man loved the pilgrim soul in you,
And loved the sorrows of your changing face;

And bending down beside the glowing bars,
Murmur, a little sadly, how Love fled
And paced upon the mountains overhead
And hid his face amid a crowd of stars.

When I read the line "But one man loved the pilgrim soul in you," I started to cry. Loudly, sobbingly. Sudsy and everyone else ignored me, perhaps used to, or fed up with, my strange ways. It was a White Spot lunch day, and as Vicki drove us there I kept up the crying jag, blubbering through a hamburger, a milk shake and our shared fries. I had no idea why I was crying, so I couldn't answer Vicki's rather unenthusiastic questions. Thereafter, throughout my high school career, just as Sudsy's voice sent me to sleep, the thought of those words— "one man loved the pilgrim soul in you, / And loved the sorrows of your changing face"—set me crying. I didn't know what a soul was (my parents were skeptics and atheists and such language was never heard in the Bell household), still less if I had one. The words bypassed my brain and leapt into my heart. When, or where, or how, was I to find the one man who would love my pilgrim soul, if indeed I had one?

- - - -

Sorting through old bags and boxes recently, I found a cache of old dresses. Why had I kept them all these years? God knows I could never fit into them now. As I laid four of them out on the bed, wisps and snatches of forgotten scenes floated into consciousness.

The Pink Hibiscus Dress: Henry

A short, bright pink sundress, a hibiscus print with a big square neck-line and collar, given to me by Henry, my first lover, when I was sixteen.

In the summer after my last year of high school (both Vicki and I were in an accelerated program where we did four years of school in three), I went to a summer camp for girls, across the border in Washington State. I was even more of a misfit than I was at Magee High in Kerrisdale. All the other girls went to private schools, like York House or Crofton House in Vancouver. A few of the girls went to a still tonier and even more expensive school, in Tacoma, Washington, called the Annie Wright Seminary. One of them, Donna, befriended me. She had been expelled from Annie Wright for letting two sailors climb up the fire escape into her room. I don't think they were playing cards.

When we returned from camp, Donna and I continued to spend time together. She was the adopted daughter of a prominent, wealthy B.C. family, and lived in the biggest house I'd ever seen, on the far side of Maple Grove Park. Her mother was having all the furniture re-upholstered after re-upholstering it six months earlier. I spent quite a bit of time there that summer. Donna's parents were plan-ning to go away for a weekend, and she secured their permission for me to stay alone in the house with her. But first her mother had to come to our house and meet my mother, to ascertain if I was a suit-able companion for Donna. Our living room, which I'd never paid any particular attention to, suddenly seemed careworn and shabby, as Donna's mother swept in on a cloud of expensive-smelling per-fume. I felt almost sorry for my own mother, who seemed to be one down in this encounter, even as I thought, surely, she should be the one questioning whether Donna was an appropriate friend for me.

Donna invited over two of her lowlife boyfriends (who we used to call "hoods"). They had both failed out of high school a few times, or were expelled, and hung out during school hours in the bleachers of Point Grey Junior High School. Donna's family had a liquor closet bigger than the size of my parents' dining room, shelves and shelves lined with the finest champagnes, wines, and single malts. Byron and Barry were in paradise. We all drank so much I don't remember the rest of the night. I woke up feeling sore between my legs, and I've always wondered if I was assaulted when I passed out on the floor.

Donna's family owned an enormous yacht, easily a hundred feet long, and I was invited to go sailing up the coast of British Columbia, again as a companion for Donna. They had a full-time chef on that boat. He was German, which felt dreamily exotic to me, and his blonde hair, blue eyes and sculpted body were catnip for my sixteen-year-old virgin (I think) self. On his off hours, he, Donna and I went swimming off the side of the boat. I was swimming in desire, too—in a semi-conscious, unfamiliar but at the same time, oddly familiar state of pure sensuality. I felt intensely alive, and for the first time in my life, beautiful. That her daughter's friend was associating with a servant clearly annoyed Donna's mother. I had no more seen social class than I had seen my own living room, and this encounter between Henry and Donna's clan was my first awareness of the inequities and prejudices of a class-based society, and of my privileged status within it.

Henry and I dated the following year. He was twenty-six, exactly ten years older than I. My father made me promise that I wouldn't go to his apartment, and every time I came home he interrogated me. "Did you go there? Look me in the eye and tell me the truth." I swore that I hadn't disobeyed him, that I hadn't set foot in that apartment. Henry and I made love on Kitsilano Beach, Locarno Beach, Spanish Banks, English Bay, Horseshoe Bay, and in the hollow tree in Stanley Park.

Henry was my first love, and I'm not sorry I chose him to be the agent of my sexual awakening and, because he was older and independent, my ticket out of my increasingly anger-fuelled household.

After my mother threw me out of the house, Henry and I got married the following spring, and spent two years at the University of British Columbia. In summer he worked for my father on Lulu Island, learning the peat moss business. We then moved to Nova Scotia, where Henry went to work reviving a moribund peat moss bog owned by my father. We spent our summers in Berwick in the Annapolis Valley, and our winters in Halifax going to Dalhousie University. He taught me how to cook, and I still occasionally make an ultra-fattening and delicious brunch dish called Kaiserschmarren, which Henry translated as "little pieces of junk fit for a king." You soak raisins in rum, then sauté them with walnuts in a whole lot of butter. Pour a rich pancake batter over this, and when it's almost cooked, cut it up into little pieces with two knives, adding a mixture of sugar and cinnamon, tossing it all together.

At sixteen, I had idolized Henry. He inhabited a world, utterly foreign to me, of working-class immigrants in Vancouver's East End. He was smart and competent and had a marvellous singing voice. During the four years we were together, we both got university degrees. At Dalhousie he played the lead in *The Mikado*, and I was cast in Albee's *The American Dream* and Pirandello's *Right You Are (If You Think You Are)*. But by the end, I began to lose respect for him. I began to come out of denial about his cheating. Reading old letters, I see that he was a bit of a blowhard, full of self-pity. And if I'm honest, I thought then, and still do now, that the pink dress was just a little cheesy.

The Ivory Mini-Dress: Michel

I've told my husband Henry I'm going to a conference; I've told Michel to meet me at the hotel, The Ritz Carleton in Montreal. He's sent ahead an enormous bouquet of white roses, and a bottle of champagne, now chilling in an ice bucket. I'm wearing a white minidress, shockingly short, with long sleeves, white satin cuffs and a long-pointed collar. It is a fuck me dress, innocent but knowing.

Michel is on his way. I ask some deity or other for forgiveness. What I'm about to do is definitive, a rupture, a rapture that will change the direction of my life. I inhale the fine aroma of the roses. There is a knock on the door. I am damned. I am free.

The Dusty Rose Dress: Victoria

The third dress is also pink, like the hibiscus dress, but another pink altogether, a kind of dusty rose, so subtle as to be almost beige, but a beige that blushes. Slim fitting, crepe, with long sleeves and a key-hole neckline, its lines are still elegance itself. This dress was given to me by Victoria, the only woman I ever fell in love with. Or rather, I've been in love with many women, but she was the only woman I loved who I also became lovers with. As a requirement of a Master's Degree in English Literature at the University of Toronto I had to pass both a French and a Latin exam, and that's how I met Victoria. She was my Latin teacher, although we were the same age. Falling for one's Latin teacher—the perfect lesbian cliché.

At the time I was reading Marx, Engels, Lenin, Mao. I remember sitting on the floor in someone's apartment with several students, including Victoria, talking about the Communist Manifesto. I said it was changing my life, it was making sense of the world. "But surely you can't understand Marx without having read Hegel," Victoria said softly. I was both furious and aroused. She had thick auburn hair, which she wore shoulder length, bluntly cut. She was an im-poverished Classics graduate student and didn't have many clothes, but those she had were of the finest materials and superbly tailored. We loved going to antique stores together, fondling old china. She bought me a pink china cup, so fine the light shone through it. I dreamt of a pearl shimmering in the bottom of the cup. More than any man I'd known, she made me feel feminine, cherished. I read her my favourite poems; she read me hers.

We called it the Virginia Woolf dress. I tried it on and stood in front of the mirror, Victoria holding my shoulders and smiling behind me. I wore it when I defended my doctoral thesis. I had to make this defense in front of six men. "They can't intimidate you if you wear this," she said, lending me a chunky no-nonsense bracelet to go with it. I managed to get through this exercise in humiliation, but then, as was customary, retired with the chair of the department to his office, to drink sherry while the committee determined the fate of the rest of my life. This man began, apropos of nothing, to recount in vivid detail sexual dreams he had had. I sweated with anger and embarrassment. It wasn't until years later, when I heard the phrase "sexual harassment" for the first time, that I could name what had happened. He was so clearly enjoying the power he wielded over me, the shame he was making me feel, as I waited for the results of my doctoral defence.

Eventually Victoria returned to her home city of Milwaukee to take up an academic position and look after the beloved aunt who had raised her. I missed her keenly for a very long time. I dreamt of her striding away from me, down Avenue Road, her dark red hair burnished in the late afternoon sun.

The Brown and Black Dress: Kenny

The last dress I unearthed is a long jersey number, with one-inch brown and black stripes running diagonally across its slinkiness, and black trim around the neck and on the cuffs. This dress I bought for myself, at Joseph Magnin's, while visiting my sister in San Francisco. There was a short two-piece version as well. I couldn't decide which one to buy, and my sister wickedly suggested getting them both. So I did, feeling self-indulgent and transgressive.

I remember it now, though, because I was wearing it when I met Kenny. We were both visiting a mutual friend in the hospital. I was wearing the short version of the dress with a dark brown felt hat that sported a saucy little pheasant feather. "I never thought I'd get a foxy woman like you to like me," he said later.

By this time, the early seventies, I was a member of the Communist Party of Canada, University of Toronto Club. I joined for a number of reasons, not least because the members of the U. of T. Club were the smartest and funniest Marxists I knew. My women friends and I were all militant feminists, viewed with suspicion by the older male power brokers in the Party, who accused us of not being sufficiently pro-working-class. They called us Revisionists; we called them Stalinists, or "dogs," short for dogmatists. Into this mix descended, from Thunder Bay, a group of working-class, hard-drinking Communist men, gay and straight. The heady cocktail of we "sophisticated" feminists and those "macho" men was irresistible. Kenny and I were inevitable. The best part was that the Stalinists didn't know how to categorize any of us any more, though not for lack of trying. The Party stalwarts were just a little hypocritical about homosexuality. They couldn't quite claim that it also was anti-working-class, because some of the macho men from Thunder Bay were openly and happily gay, but they wished they could. This was, incidentally, the hill I chose to die on. When I left the Party after six years, it was because of their stance, or lack of a stance, on homosexuality—the same reason I joined the Anglican and not the Catholic church many years later.

——

Kenny was a Grade Seven dropout; I was writing my doctoral dissertation at York University. He was smart, quick-witted, funny and outrageous. We partied every weekend, drinking, smoking pot and dancing all night to the Rolling Stones. Monday mornings, grievously hungover, I'd be back in my carrel at the university library. He walked into a party late one night and called out: "Well I'd like to fuck all youse women, but I think I'll get drunk instead."

We all laughed. He was Kenny. Sex was simple, joyous and plentiful. He sincerely wanted to understand and support feminism. "If I say something wrong, just feel free to crush my nuts," he was fond of saying. Out bike riding once, and coasting downhill, I put my legs straight out in front of me and let go of the handlebars, whooping in an ecstasy of happiness. Kenny often referred to this scene. He celebrated my sense of abandonment. He always averred that when we got old he would run a sex home for seniors. Kenny thought that old people not having sex (or so he thought) was a terrible social injustice.

He too moved away, back to Thunder Bay and a successful contracting business. I just assumed I would see him again some day, and we would talk over old times together, but last fall, a few minutes before I was to go on stage and give a talk about my current art exhibition, I got a text saying he'd died suddenly of a heart attack. RIP Kenny Van Male. He got a vasectomy before I met him and planned to change his name to Kenny Van Neuter.

My sister married at twenty-three and stayed married to the same man until his death when she was eighty-six. I walked a different road. There were other lovers, other relationships. Did I find that "one man" who would love my inner self? I think everyone who has loved me has loved the pilgrim soul in me. Maybe it's the aggregate of all these loves that brought the pilgrim soul into being, or perhaps uncovered it, disrobed it. When the greatest love of my life, Terry McAuliffe, died of brain cancer, any doubts about whether I had a soul were washed away by years of relentless grief, leaving me sure of only one thing. I don't have a soul; I am a soul. My life itself a pilgrimage.

POSTSCRIPT

A year or two after Terry died, I was talking to a young man at a party, a singer-songwriter from Vancouver. He asked me what high school I'd gone to, and it transpired that he was my old pal Vicki Berner's nephew, the son of her car-lending brother. He told me Vicki had eventually given up tennis for golf. In 1961, she was the youngest athlete at the Maccabiah Games in Israel, winning the tennis gold medal; now she was about to compete as the oldest athlete in the Maccabiah Games, in women's golf. He gave me her number and we spoke on the phone. She didn't remember *The Catcher in the Rye*, or this: we were reading *Julius Caesar* in school, and had to memorize a short four-line passage. For unknown reasons, we chanted these lines over and over every day as we headed from Magee to my house on Cypress Street for cigarettes, pool, and lunch, marching in time to the iambic pentameter, and shouting out the punctuation as loud as we could:

These GROWing FEAThers PLUCK'd from Caesar's WING
Will MAKE him FLY an ORDinary PITCH **COMMA!**
Who ELSE would SOAR aBOVE the VIEW of MEN
And KEEP us ALL in SERvile fearfulNESS **PERIOD!!!**

I recently looked up Vicki and found her obituary. She had a long career in various roles for the American tennis community, and died in 2017 after a short illness. She won the gold medal for golf at the Maccabiah Games in 2005.

HOW I DIDN'T
BECOME A MAOIST

My father had a good friend from his Air Force days named John D., whom he always held up as the very exemplar of an honest man. John D. was a commercial fisherman who plied the cold waters of northern British Columbia, and knew the crannies and shoals of the coast like a deft, experienced lover. He was a type—an old CCFer, gruff, laconic and kind. His work was seasonal, and every winter he went sport fishing for a few weeks in Mexico. Unlike his fishermen buddies, he cancelled his unemployment benefits for the weeks he was on holiday. For this reason, my father deemed him to be the paragon of honesty.

He had two sons, Paul, and Robert, roughly my age, and an estranged, or perhaps divorced, wife (such things weren't spoken of in front of children then) who had committed some sin people whispered about out of our hearing. Aptly, she was named Trixie. Somehow, John was managing to raise Paul and Robert on his own.

Years later, when I was a graduate student in the English department at the University of Toronto, I was living with Larry Hoffman in an apartment on Robert Street. Larry was a prominent campus radical, a Jewish draft dodger from Brooklyn with long curly black hair and a significant moustache. I learned a lot about left wing politics from Larry as we smoked dope every night, and I listened as he plotted the revolution.

One day I got a call from my father.

"Robin, you remember my good friend John D.? His boys, Paul, and Robert are both living in Toronto now. I've given them your phone number. They're both involved in left wing politics so I think you'll have a lot in common."

The boys duly appeared on our doorstep and Paul started dropping by quite frequently. They had both joined the Communist Party of Canada (Marxist-Leninist), which followed the line of China and Mao Tse-tung (as it was spelled at the time), as distinct from the plain Communist Party of Canada, which followed the line of the Soviet Union. Members of the CPC (ML) were known as the Maoists. (Not to be confused with Trotskyites, known to everyone else as the Trots.)

Of the many Maoist slogans and posters, I especially liked the one featuring a drawing of Trudeau with his hair like Madame de Pompadour and the headline: "Pierre Elliott Trudeau: Prince of Lackeys!" At every election they plastered the campus and surroundings with posters admonishing "Don't vote—they're all the same," a slogan gladly taken up by young women who were beginning then, in the late sixties, to become feminists. The Maoists' favourite slogan, though, was "blood debts will be paid in blood." Paul was particularly fond of that one and dropped it into any conversation, as casually as if he'd been talking about the weather.

Now, I would guess that the CPC (ML), the Maoists, probably had at most a thousand, maybe two thousand, members in the whole country. Their leader, based in Vancouver, was named Hardial Bains; known to us as "hardly any brains." Yet the Party had a daily newspaper, *The People's Canada Daily News*, copies of which Paul liked to drop over to us. Larry and I loved reading it while stoned, laughing so hard we had to hold our stomachs. Someone threw a brick through the window of the Maoist bookstore in Halifax. (They also seemed to have bookstores in every major city.) "Blood debts will be paid in blood" screamed the headline. One day I asked Paul how they could put out a paper every day. "Oh, it's easy," he said. "We just use the slogans and plug in the story." Once he brought us the Quebec issue, with its blaring headline: "Les Dettes de Sang seront payées en Sang!"

I was becoming increasingly involved in the left and in feminism, going to meetings and demonstrations, growing my hair long and wearing it in braids, sporting plaid shirts, jeans, and work boots. Sometimes I switched this outfit up for a silk shirt, an off-white leather micro miniskirt my sister had sent me from Berkeley, and strands and strands of beads.

My friend Ken still likes to tell this story about Larry and me. Ken was working as a bartender at the University of Toronto Graduate Students' Union, a hotbed of lefty plotting, strategizing and vicious political arguments. We strode up to the bar and ordered two Calgary Exports. "Why Calgary Exports?" Ken asked, amazed. "Well, Labatts is owned by Brascan," I explained, "and they're destroying the rain forest [this was fifty years ago]; and Molson's is on strike and we're supporting the workers by boycotting them. So that leaves Calgary Export. You think we drink this shit because we like it?"

I wanted to learn more about Marx, Engels, Lenin and Mao and asked Phyllis Clarke if she would lead a study group. Phyllis had returned in her late forties to do a PhD in Political Science. She had left in her late twenties, after her MA. Back then she was working part time as a teaching assistant for her thesis supervisor, Harold Innis. Innis was the author of *The Fur Trade in Canada*, a deadly dull but very influential book for campus lefties, and the source of most of Marshall McLuhan's ideas about communication theory. One day Innis called her into his office.

"Phyllis, I can't write the letter of recommendation you need to enter the doctoral program."

"Why not?" she asked, "I'm your top student!"

"First of all, you're Jewish, and there's a quota for Jewish students. Second, you're a Communist, and no one will hire you. But most of all, it's because you're a woman!" So she went off to Regina, married Nelson Clarke, and worked as a Party organizer for twenty years.

How thrilled she must have been when I asked her to lead a Marxist study group. But Phyllis, who smoked constantly and drank several scotches of an evening, was not one to show her feelings. Our group met in the late afternoon at that same Graduate Students' Union on Willcocks Street. It was filled with comfortable old armchairs and sofas, and every few feet there was a hanging basket with a houseplant. There were five or six of us, including a tall, taciturn graduate student who later transferred to the Royal Military College in Kingston. I figured he was the cop in the group. We assumed that every left-wing meeting had at least one spy.

Phyllis calmly and effectively refuted all my cherished New Left opinions.

"Why can't we function with consensus? Why do we need leaders? Isn't hierarchy what we want to get rid of?"

"That just isn't efficient enough. We need a democratic process, otherwise we'll debate until the cows come home. These so-called 'struggle sessions' that the Maoists believe in are often just a not very subtle form of bullying."

"But why do we need a revolutionary party? Why can't we just overturn the state en masse? Wouldn't that be more democratic?"

"It was Lenin who said that in order to make a revolution, you need a revolutionary party. You need organization, coordination, leadership, discipline. Castro believed the same. And they both achieved revolutions in Russia and Cuba."

We knew that the session was over when Nelson walked in and Phyllis commanded, in her hoarse smoker's voice: "Nelson, get me a drink!"

Eventually, through Phyllis's reasoned arguments, and by studying the history of Marxism and of the Russian Revolution, I was won over. I did indeed believe that you can't make a revolution without a revolutionary party. In the early seventies, in the small but influential left-wing circles at the University of Toronto, the word quickly got out that I was looking to join something. I was low-hanging political fruit. Various groups on campus began to court me. I was invited to meetings by the University of Toronto Communist Club, various Trotskyite sects, and the Canadian Liberation Movement.

The Maoists on campus, through none other than Robert D., invited me to be one of their noon hour guest speakers. They assured me I could choose any topic. I decided to give a talk on Frantz Fanon, whose book *Black Skin White Masks* I had been reading, and which I thought was revelatory. (I still do.) I walked into the small, windowless, airless classroom in Sidney Smith Hall, where the lunchtime series was held, and after being introduced, began to speak.

"Fanon believed there was a kind of internalized colonialism, that Black Africans wore a mask, and the task of organizing is also a psychological task, to uncover the true, authentic self, unmediated by colonialism (the white mask)," I said. (Even at this early, rather dogmatic, stage in my Marxist thinking, I was drawn to ideas about consciousness, psychology, art, and creativity.)

There were about twenty people in the audience, sitting at desks, and I noticed they were, with one or two exceptions, all men. I had spoken for no more than three minutes when on some invisible signal, all twenty members of the audience stood up as one, waved their little red books in the air, and denounced me—*their invited speaker.*

"Bourgeois!"
"Imperialist!"
"Feminist!"
"Enemy of the people!"
"Running dog lackey!"

The look in some of those eyes was definitely unhinged. I was furious, and also a little frightened, as I made my way carefully through the chanting crowd and finally, with relief, out the door.

So I didn't become a Maoist. I didn't join their Communist Party of Canada (Marxist-Leninist).

A year or two after my public shaming, I became friends with a man who was putting himself through a PhD in Political Science by working as a parole officer. He had several friends who were RCMP officers. One night over drinks one of them said to Carl, apropos of the Maoists, "If we pulled out of that organization it would be dead by tomorrow morning."

They were crazy times, and much of it seems silly in hindsight, no less because we were so deadly serious. I knew that some of the Maoists were more or less lunatics, so why did I agree to their invitation to speak at their lunchtime series? As I look back, I think I was driven by two ideas, and those two ideas have stayed with me all my life.

First, I wanted to prove that Jesus Christ was wrong about poverty. In Matthew 26, the Evangelist tells the story of how Jesus was eating with his disciples when a woman (presumably a wealthy one) anointed his head with very expensive oil poured from an alabaster jug. His disciples remonstrated with him, saying it would have been better to sell the pricey oil and give the money to the poor. "The poor you will always have with you," Jesus said. And so far, he's been right, and he's just as right now as he ever was over the last 2,000 years.

But reading Marx convinced me that there is progress in human history, that the inevitable progression from capitalism to socialism was obvious if you consider the inevitable progression from feudalism to capitalism. The world, heretofore completely confusing and opaque to me, suddenly made sense. The way to prove Jesus wrong was to make a revolution and create economic equality. Justice for all! Expropriate the expropriators! Workers of the world, unite!

I don't know if I still believe in progress. The twentieth century had more wars, and more devastating wars, than the previous 500 years combined. The gap between the rich few and the poor many increases hourly, throwing millions upon millions in the developing world into desperate poverty, and gutting jobs and livelihoods in North America. Climate Armageddon will certainly affect poor people in poor countries more than it will affect well off people in countries like ours; still, even in wealthier countries it will make a lot of people much poorer. And yet—and yet—after a decades-long hiatus, I'm marching again: women's marches, climate marches. Against all reason, I hold onto hope that in some form of modified socialism, we can create equality, we can prove Jesus wrong—the poor will not always be with us. And we can do so using his own words in that same gospel (Matthew 25):

> For I was hungry, and you gave me something to eat, I was thirsty and you gave me something to drink, I was a stranger and you invited me in, I needed clothes and you clothed me, I was sick and you looked after me, I was in prison and you came to visit me. Truly I tell you, whatever you did for one of the least of these brothers and sisters of mine, you did for me.

The second idea that motivated me to give a lunch hour talk about Frantz Fanon to those red-book-waving politicos was a desire, however badly placed, to feel part of something bigger than myself. Eventually, recruited by Phyllis Clarke, I did join a somewhat saner left-wing political party. For about a decade I had the gratifying feeling that my words and actions mattered, that the collective was so much more than what I could do as a lone person. I genuinely thought that we had the right answers, and we simply needed to put them on placards and people would join the revolutionary movement.

Also it was always fun and interesting to hang out at that bar of the Graduate Students' Union, even after I left the University of Toronto. I think my half-Jewish DNA loved the parry and thrust, the "gotchas" and witty comebacks, of our political debates. Eventually, however, I began to wonder if our angry, placard-waving, slogan-chanting demonstrations weren't in some way just feeding those we opposed, giving energy to the anger of the forces of power in a strange kind of political Moebius strip. I began to question the politics of anger, and to question why creativity wasn't made a central part of our thinking and our struggle. I read and re-read Antonio Gramsci, to my mind the most enlightened and imaginative of all Marxists. It was my own creativity that was being stifled, creativity and imagination that lay dormant under all the layers of academic and Marxist thinking.

So I wrote an article for the Feminist journal *Fireweed* called "Why I Left the Left to Write."

And there was still the call to something other, something vaguely transcendent. It was an ache, a longing. To the dismay of my lefty friends, I started to explore New Age spirituality and spent some years in Big Sur, California. Through many twists and turns, I found my way towards a conflicted and complicated belief in God and in Christianity, and, much to my own surprise, became a regular churchgoer. But this wasn't an "answer." The yearning continues. It's the yearning itself that is the belief; longing that is the essence of faith. That's what's meant by "seek and ye shall find"; it's the seeking, not the finding. God is in the wanting.

I've met progressive men and women doing heartening and effective political work, some of them nuns and monks. They work with refugees, are climate activists and critics of capitalism. Their politics are not motivated by anger; they are motivated by love. I don't hold up placards any more with the correct slogan, there's no "blood debts will be paid in blood." I've come to embrace a politics of reverence for the creation, and love and justice for its threatened and most vulnerable inhabitants.

IN DEINE HÄNDE

3a. A Prie A

In deine Hände befehl ich meinen
Geist; du hast mich erlöset, Herr,
du getreuer Gott. (Psalm 31:6)
J.S. Bach, from Cantata 106

3a. Aria A

Into Your hands I commit my
spirit; you have redeemed me,
Lord, faithful God.

1. "I feel defined by my losses. I feel marked. I feel like Job.
It's a loss of social space, of belonging."

Terry and I went to Emergency at Toronto Western Hospital at noon
in mid September, 2002. He had been complaining of tingling in
the left side of his mouth, and then he lost his balance and began
lurching from side to side. We waited twelve hours. At midnight, we
were told that he had a brain tumour. I took a step, and crossed the
border into another country, a country with no street signs, no geo-
graphical landmarks, for which there was no map. I looked everywhere, and then I saw a solitary person: my friend Dayne was there.
He knew this landscape intimately, and he would be my Virgil in
the land of sickness, death, and mourning.

Dayne and I were friends for many years and held each other's
hands through various relationship dramas and traumas. Then he
found Gary, and I found Terry, and the four of us became close

couple friends. We had elaborate dinner parties, watched movies together, went to concerts.

Dayne came from a working-class family of eight children in Moncton, New Brunswick. His father had a violent temper and his mother beat the children regularly. "There was so much violence and shame in my family. But so much love as well." His oldest brother was convicted for dealing drugs and hanged himself in prison. That's when Dayne stopped drinking and found a spiritual calling in sobriety.

One of his sisters once told me: "In a big family, the older children raise the younger ones." Dayne's youngest brother, Danny, a gifted photographer, died of AIDS. "Danny was my baby," Dayne sobbed. "He was MY baby!"

When he was twelve he saw a notice for a concert in the school gymnasium—Maureen Forrester and Lois Marshall. This was in the very early days of the Canada Council, founded on the recommendation of the Massey Report on Culture, when they sponsored artists to tour all over Canada. Dayne took himself to the school. Maureen Forrester sailed into her spotlight and bowed. Then this small woman, using braces on both legs, made her way painstakingly across the stage. Lois Marshall began to sing. Dayne said when she opened her mouth, he immediately knew two things: that he was gay, and that he would leave Moncton. Danny would follow him to Toronto, where we all met.

2. "In the aftermath of each death there's this profound disruption. The need to go on living is a burden for me. I just want to go to sleep. It's too much to bear."

Another brother hanged himself. A sister who struggled with mental illness was sent home from the hospital, told she was imagining her symptoms. Hours later she was dead from a bronchial infection. Of the eight siblings, four pre-deceased him. As well as his brother Danny, he lost many former lovers and many dear friends to AIDS.

3. "It's a desire to join the loved one."

Terry received treatment in the Gerry and Nancy Pencer Brain Tumour Centre on the eighteenth floor of Princess Margaret Hospital. (Gerry Pencer was a wealthy Canadian financier who also died of brain cancer.) There were always beautiful arrays of flowers, fresh fruit, and delicious baked goods. Comfortable sofas and armchairs. If you were dying of a brain tumour, this was the place to be. Before cell phones were ubiquitous, there were several phones; you could call long distance to anywhere in the world. One day after one of Terry's radiation treatments, we were "relaxing" in the Pencer Centre. I picked up the phone and called Dayne. I was crying so hard he could barely make out what I was saying. "Terry just had radiation. They make this wire mesh mask contoured to his face, and they bolt it down so he can't move. He's so brave, I could never be that brave. And also my little kitten is dying. I'm going to have to go home and take him to the vet and have him euthanized. And there was this little four-year-old boy in the radiation pod next to Terry. It's essential that you lie completely still for the radiation. He was terrified, screaming. His parents were talking to him through a microphone, trying to get him to be still. 'Lie still, lie still,' they begged him over and over and over. His screams felt like they were inside my head. I don't think I can stand this. I don't think I can endure it."

There was a long pause. Then, "I love you, Robin," was all he said. All I needed and wanted to hear. What else was there to say?

4. "It rips away filters and veils. People avoid people who are grieving. Because they're afraid."

After Terry died, the mornings were the worst. I woke up feeling bolted to the bed myself, not by a mask, but by dread. I couldn't talk to anyone, I didn't have words. I remember the first spring, when the world coming back to life was a kind of agony to me, because Terry wasn't coming back with it. The "force that through the green fuse drives the flower" sliced through my heart. Eventually, almost every day, I ended up calling Dayne. "Yes," he said, "I know just how you feel. Spring can be the hardest time of the year. There's a comfort in the fall when everything is dying. Also, I think you should try and get up, take a shower, put some clothes on. It will help, I promise."

5. *"Loss keeps telling me how to let go."*

It wasn't all about grief and loss. Dayne had a wild and wicked sense of humour. He teased me relentlessly, made me laugh in the midst of both of us crying. Once, we were sitting across from each other in a restaurant. I was wearing a low cut top that laced up the front, and, as usual, bawling. Dayne reached over and loosened the laces. "There, now there's more room for your heaving breast, Brünnhilde." Of course, I burst out laughing.

6. *"The music is like a communion for me. It creates a space where I can be with everyone, the living and the dead."*

One of the art projects I did after Terry died was called *Marks in the River of Time.* I invited eighty people I knew to come to my studio and allow me to videotape them talking about loss in their life, and how it had changed them. I asked them to bring me a gift, and a piece of music.

Dayne's interview took place on World AIDS Day, December 1, 2005, in the recent aftermath of the death of his sister Susan, the fourth of his siblings to die. The quotations in this essay are transcribed from that videotape. The music Dayne brought was the Bach cantata *In Deine Hände.* The gift was a beautiful, shimmery piece of cloth that had belonged to Danny. As he gave me the cloth, we played the music, and danced with the cloth, passing it back and forth, our hands moving with the glittering black material, in time to the Bach cantata.

Dayne and Gary had a house in Nova Scotia, near Shelburne on the South Shore. Eight months after we danced with Bach and Danny's cloth, Dayne died of a heart attack while he was in his garden. The coroner said he was probably dead before his head hit the ground, so there's that. I flew to Halifax, rented a car, and met Gary at the funeral parlour. I was able to see Dayne one last time, and say goodbye. I put Danny's cloth tenderly over him; it was cremated with him.

I think it is possible to die of a broken heart.

7. *"And just to be grateful."*

I was asked to speak about Dayne's spirituality at the memorial service held in Toronto. I told this story: I once asked Dayne, in a most serious and urgent tone, if he believed in God. "Praise the Lord and pass the K-Y Jelly!" he shouted gleefully, cackling his crazy laugh. I also said that regardless of what he believed, his actions left us this legacy: no matter how many and how painful his losses, he never stopped loving, and he never stopped laughing.

––––

POSTSCRIPT

Excerpt from *Rocky Night in Canada* by Dayne Ogilvie and Robin Pacific

Some background: I came to the conclusion, in my late twenties, that romantic relationships between men and women were, in a word, fucked. I decided that I would remove all emotion from sexuality and treat it like a pure physical need. Expunge any and all feelings from sexual encounters with men.

I set out to achieve this by going to parties by myself, getting drunk and/or stoned, waiting until very late, and picking up a random man on the dance floor. Then we'd go back to his place and have sex. These men lived in sad and lonely apartments; there was always a single plate and a glass drying on the drain rack. I'd go home before morning, in case I might wake up with an emotion, in case I felt a scintilla of longing, caring, or even liking. My campaign was very effective. I had lots of mediocre sex, but my heart was intact. Or so I thought.

The film script Dayne and I wrote together was about the relationship between a gay man somewhat obsessed with sex (Gregory, based on Dayne) and a single mother, also obsessed with sex (Marla, based on me). Both of them spend most of their time trying, unsuccessfully, to get laid. Marla is a raving, ranting Marxist feminist who believes in the material economics of sex. She's separated from Jeff, the uptight father of their four-year-old daughter, Willow. Gregory is her best friend, romantic, sentimental and, like Dayne, out and loud and proud.

Marla organizes her sex life by earning money doing telephone sex two nights a week and hiring a male prostitute one night a week. His fees are approximately double what she charges; so much for the demand for equal pay for equal work. Not that it was equal; all he had to do was get and keep an erection. Marla had a more demanding job, since telephone sex requires a strong narrative sense—the ability to make up convincing stories with a story arc, a climax, and a denouement. The male prostitute, who we called Rocky, became a character in our movie.

Both Marla and Gregory find sexual happiness in radically different ways. I wrote Marla's lines, and Dayne wrote Gregory's.

SCENE 51:

Interior. Marla's apartment. Day.

Marla is again on the phone.

MARLA: Home Entertainment Inc.? I was looking for someone to come over and visit for a few hours, Saturday.

VOICE: Well, I'm just the one you're looking for. I'm 6 feet tall, 185 pounds, dark hair, dark eyes, and 7 between my legs.

MARLA: Inches or centimeters?

VOICE: I charge $70 per hour.

MARLA: (*doodling: $70 for 7 inches = $10 per inch*) Hmmm, I was thinking maybe two hours, how about $100 for two hours?

VOICE: (*pause*) Sure.

SCENE 52:

Interior. Marla's apartment. Evening.

It's another warm summer night. Gregory and his new lover Michael, from the Big Turnip, approach Marla's door, which is open. Gregory knocks, not too loudly, and enters. They hear Marla's voice coming from the bedroom.

MARLA: (*groaning orgasmically*) Oooooohhhhhh. Are you coming? Oh, I want you to come! Oh my God, it's so hard, it's so big, are you coming now? Oh you make me feel so good.

We hear another muffled voice. Marla hears the door, pushes open the bedroom door with one hand and gestures, covering the mouthpiece, whispers:

MARLA: Be with you in a minute, I'm on the phone.

Gregory and his pal freeze. Gregory shrugs, walks in, starts his domestic ritual of cleaning up Willow's toys, stacking dirty dishes, wiping the table. He puts on a record. Marla emerges.

MARLA: Perfect timing, I just finished. (*Nodding to Michael, who she hasn't met*) Hi. Gregory, how often do people have sex? On the average. In Canada.

GREGORY: *(Blushing, looking at Michael)* Twice a night?

MARLA: Twice a week, Gregory, just two times a week. So that's what I'm doing. Thursdays and Saturdays. I've decided to be normal.

GREGORY: Cup of tea? This is Michael, by the way. Michael, meet Marla.

MARLA: Hi. I'd love some tea.

MICHAEL: Hi.

GREGORY: Who was that on the phone?

MARLA: How should I know? Gregory, I just have to tell you, I've found THE PERFECT LOVER.

GREGORY: Marla, that's incredible. SO HAVE I! (*He puts one arm around Marla and the other around Michael.*) We met at the Big Turnip. Does he know his vegetables!

MARLA: His name is Rocky. Every Saturday night, Gregory, it's Rocky Night in Canada. I've finally solved the problem— I've created sexual communism BEFORE the revolution.

GREGORY: More tea?

MARLA: What do you pay a therapist? What do you pay for a great hair cut? Let's face it, $100 is a good deal for a great lay, and sometimes he stays longer than the two hours.

GREGORY: Marla, this is love?

MARLA: But naturally, I can't afford it, so on Thursdays, I do telephone sex fantasies. I get $20 a shot, takes about 2 ½ hours —communism! To each according to her need, from each according to her ability. Rocky's got 7 between his legs, and I've got an MA in Sociology. It fits into my schedule perfectly —I do it on the nights Jeff has Willow, and it never interferes with my writing!

HOW I BECAME
AN ARTIST

I looked around the circle of eager faces. These were the Pelican Players, c. 1982. We were sitting on the floor in the parish hall of St. Chad's Anglican Church at Dufferin and St. Clair in Toronto. The priest, whose surname was also Chad, had rented it to us for peanuts five days a week.

"OK, excellent work everyone. Let's take a break. On your lunch hour I'd like each of you to observe someone in the neighbourhood—how they talk, how they move their hands, their facial expressions, how they walk. And present them after the break. And oh —Diana, could you write a song please for Scene 6, about inflation? I don't need it until the end of the week."

After lunch, Diana sang a song called "The High Cost of Oranges Blues" she'd written on the break. Alison did a monologue as an Italian grocer that had us all in stitches.

"Where did you find this guy?" I asked. "Oh, I just made him up," she said. Alison Sealy Smith, before returning to Barbados to head their Cultural Foundation, became a well-known Toronto actor and spent two seasons at the Stratford Festival. Diana Braithwaite still performs as a blues artist and has won numerous awards, including a Lifetime Achievement Award and Best Songwriter Award at the Maple Blues Awards.

I wrote my doctoral dissertation on different models of political theatre—how theatre artists tried to make art that would change the world. When I couldn't get an academic job, I went on unemployment insurance for six months and wrote a couple of plays. I was also reading the Italian Communist Antonio Gramsci, who believed the task of the "organic intellectual" was to find ways for people to transform themselves from passive *consumers* of culture into active *producers* of culture.

This idea took root in me and grew into all aspects of my artistic life. I looked at different theatre movements, from German Expressionism in the twenties, to anti-nuclear peace activists and the "angry young men" playwrights in England in the fifties, to the growing pride in our national history made into collective creation theatre by Theatre Passe Muraille and others in Canada. I decided I would form a theatre company based on Gramsci's idea. We would do only original collective creations; the actors in the company would become the playwrights, and I would be the director. I had no training in theatre, playwrighting, or directing. #flyingbytheseatofherpants.

The theatre company was called Pelican Players. I hired aspiring young actors on Employment Canada Grants. Yes, I became an expert at persuading government bureaucrats that theatre training would help young people in job interviews. For this I received enough funding to run the company for a year. Those were the days, my friend.

I wasn't interested in a typical theatre audience—mostly white, middle class, middle aged—so we performed in libraries, churches, and parks. My Gramscian vision came to life as scenes, monologues and songs seemed to flood out from the exercises I gave the group.

As good as it was, in retrospect, I remember how fragile my ego was then, how uncertain my sense of how a play actually worked. I put up a front of competence ("Yes, that's great, keep that line"), but inwardly I was possessed by a numbing insecurity. Only in the rehearsal hall, and during a performance, was I able to let go of the shame, the fear of exposure, that tormented me. After the run of a play, these feelings were so acute I often didn't leave the house for days. So, even as our popularity and acclaim grew, when the few inevitable unfavourable reviews appeared in journals, I collapsed. I was accused in print, by both white and Black writers, of being a racist, of running a hierarchical company, as a white director working with Black actors.

At the same time, I was writing and performing my own scripts. I made a piece called *Integrated Circuits* about women and writing, feminism, and place. I talked about my homesickness for British Columbia, and the racism against Indigenous people prevalent when I was a child there. I performed it at a conference in Vancouver called *Women and Words*. My ironic stance about racism was misconstrued as racism itself, and I was met with silence, no applause, and some scattered boos. I wanted to crawl away and hide, and hide I did—a friend of a friend loaned me a cabin for a few days, and I sat there abjectly, drinking scotch and alternately raging and crying. I had been publicly humiliated, and I didn't know how I would ever walk that back.

Pelican Players, meanwhile, continued to perform and be enthusiastically received. I hired a "dream cast" of five of the most gifted of our actors. We created a play called *Dear Cherry, Remember the Ginger Wine*, and Diana Braithwaite wrote a two-hander for herself and Alison called *Martha and Elvira*. We took these two plays to London, England, to LIFT (London International Festival of Theatre) and to the Edinburgh Fringe Festival. They were hugely popular, but I was falling deeper and deeper into a morose, bleak despair.

I put my tail between my legs and left Toronto for Big Sur, California, where I had been taking occasional workshops at the Esalen Institute, the epicentre of New Age spiritual practices. I didn't think I'd ever direct or write a play again. The very nature of language itself felt like a source of shame; I felt as if my skin had come off. Once again, I needed to hide.

And it was possible to hide amidst the wild assortment of spiritual seekers there, from enlightened leaders (Alan Watts, Baba Ram Dass, Jessica Britt to name a few), to the New Age version of snake oil salesmen. I did some rather astonishing sessions with a Brazilian woman there, Maria Lucia Sauer, who was a self-proclaimed psychic and healer. She was training some of the people at Esalen in her techniques and asked for a volunteer for her acolytes to practice on.

I lay on the floor. (There weren't many chairs at Esalen, just giant pillows. John Upledger, the father of Craniosacral Therapy, was renowned for asking: "Is the New Age over? Can someone please bring me a chair?") Twenty people put their hands lightly on my body and channeled their healing energy to me. Regardless of what I believed then—or believe now—it was a singularly powerful experience. I felt an oceanic sense of calm and peace. For once my non-stop babbling ego, telling me all the ways I'd failed, all the ways I was a bad person, just shut up. Slowly, like an image becoming clear in a steamed up bathroom mirror, I began to see words as three-dimensional objects, with weight, depth, colour. I saw these words: *Africa Married Greece Buried Africa.* There was an art barn at Esalen, and I started going there and painting the words on giant sheets of paper, one sheet for each of the five words.

Gradually, I began to define myself as a visual artist rather than a writer. Writing was so hard, it felt like I had to squeeze the words out of my psyche, like a jammed-up ketchup bottle; I procrastinated endlessly and hated myself for it. But the self-doubt and pain of trying to write melted away when I began to play with images. Once again, I had no training, so I started making collages, using texts and images and rubber stamps. It felt like playing; I was a child again. When I eventually returned to Toronto I took life drawing classes for a few years at the Toronto School of Art. This was a struggle indeed, as I have no natural ability and certainly no experience. But the teachers there, all practicing artists themselves, encouraged and nurtured me and assured me that technique could be learned, but what I had, namely ideas, was unique and unteachable. As soon as I was able to execute a reasonable drawing, I left and embarked on my path as a visual artist, spending twenty-five years making paintings, drawings, videos, web-based projects, performances, installations, and large-scale community art projects.

There were, of course, many roadblocks and problems along the way, particularly with community art projects. I often seemed to incur the anger of the participants. Perhaps I was dictatorial, undiplomatic, not gentle enough. However, I do believe that dragons guard the gates of creativity, and often when people approach those gates for the first time, some fury is unleashed. And that fury sometimes attached to me. In retrospect, I don't think I made a safe enough container for newly born creativity.

I organized a project with ex-prisoners in a halfway house; men who'd served time for violent crimes, including armed robbery, pedophilia, and sexual assault. I asked each of eighteen residents how they wanted to be remembered and, if they left a gift behind, what it would be. I was working on the principle that these men were more than the crimes they'd committed. Three of the residents were very gifted artists. They made drawings of the 'gifts' of each resident; I silkscreened some of their words, and secured exhibition space at Toronto City Hall.

As the exhibition deadline neared, the project wobbled back and forth. There were threats of shutting the show down from the powers that be in Corrections Canada. (One of the inmates made an unflattering comment about Stephen Harper, Canada's then Prime Minister.) The three artists I was working with stalled and couldn't meet their deadlines. (As a friend said, if they were practising the seven habits of highly successful people, they wouldn't be in the halfway house in the first place.)

I planned to tour the exhibit to churches and restorative justice conferences, but after the City Hall show, in a big and very confrontational meeting, some of the inmates accused me of trying to sell the artworks and keep the money for myself. These were men who a week before I had thought were friends. Nothing I or the chaplain I was working with said could counter this idea, so the works were returned to the artists and the inmates, and within a few months were destroyed or otherwise disappeared. It wasn't a pleasant experience, that meeting. I did realize later, when my feathers became unruffled, that these were men who could actually lose their lives if they trusted the wrong person.

I cite this example, but there were others, and looking back I realize I didn't work slowly enough. I barged into communities I didn't know. There wasn't sufficient infrastructure to support the work. Impatience is my besetting sin. Just because I like working without a net doesn't mean I should expect that of others.

When it works, though, nothing is more wonderful or satisfying to me than community art. I worked with twenty security guards at the Art Gallery of Ontario and created an exhibit throughout the gallery that showcased them with their words and life-size photographs. The project took a year and a half, and I came to know the participants well. I had the support of the institution. Whenever I saw artistic talent among the guards, I found ways to incorporate their work, including having one guard, Angus Muller, take all the photographs, and two musicians perform at the opening. We celebrated after the show came down with an excellent bottle of tequila and appreciation all around. To this day, if I go to the gallery and see one of them working, I get a big hug.

So there has been misery and there has been joy. I made up a system called "Robin's Unified Theory of Artistic Production," which goes something like this. There are three stages to the creation of a work: (1) the making of it, (2) the dissemination of it, and (3) the aftermath. Any one of those stages can be misery or bliss. There are eight possible permutations. The chances of a project being bliss/bliss/bliss are one in eight, as are the chances of it being misery/misery/misery. It's pretty nearly always some combination. Artists often become depressed after a show ends, or an exhibition comes down. I usually love making the work, even if it's a struggle, but afterwards I still sometimes meet my old friends Shame and Fear of Exposure. Happily, as I age, they've become more muted, or at least shorter-lived.

I never actually left language behind. I'm fascinated by the boundaries and the marriages of images and words. Books themselves are art materials. I made a river of two thousand books in the Cedarvale Ravine in Toronto, the edges of their pages painted blue by children in the local Parks and Recreation program. The books made a single, sinuous line, following the course of the buried Castle Frank Brook, a tributary to the Don River. In the video of the installation, I ask, "Did language bury nature?"

I collected books by their titles: times of the day, the seasons, the elements and so on, then put them by category in a wheelbarrow and walked up and down the street giving them away, photographing each person holding their book. So the titles told a story. I made a shamanic cloak out of the dyed-red pages of Marx and Engels books, and a giant headdress made to look like the Tatlin Tower, the famous but never built monument to the Third International, and wore them at various street festivals.

Then one day, my new and now, sadly, late friend, Diana Meredith, told me about a writing group she was in, run by her husband. Without thinking about it, I asked if I could join. I fell into that group like I'd been there for years. I reached back to my younger self and stitched up all the years in between. The anguish and shame of those early years as a writer are (mostly) gone. Writing is physically so much less demanding than the art projects I cook up, but it still supplies the adrenalin jolt of joy I find in any creative endeavour. Occasionally the perfect phrase will pop into my head, unbidden. Where did it come from? It arrives fully formed, like a baby.

From playwright and theatre director to visual artist, to writer— no matter the struggles with the world and my own nature, some-how the creative drive pushed me through. For the last ten years, I've gone once a month to see a Spiritual Director, a Capuchin friar who wears his wisdom lightly and has a lovely sense of humour. "I don't seem to pray very much these days," I've said a few times. "Whenever you are being creative, you are in prayer," he says.

Once I asked Jeff, who occasionally walks my Samoyed soul-mate Mercy, if I could go out on a walk with him and his dogs. He took all of us to a big industrial park in the far west end of the city. It was an April day, with that sense of early spring potentiality, everything misty and grey-green. Mercy was clearly very proud that I was there and, I could swear, lorded it over the other dogs. It re-minded me of going on school field trips with my daughter. Jeff was in his element, herding and encouraging and letting them all run free. The next time he arrived to pick her up, I said, "How lucky we are, the ones for whom their work is also their calling." He looked at me oddly, and then he nodded.

HOW I BECAME A "CHRISTIAN"

Sometimes I wonder what my friends—particularly my artist friends, and especially my political friends—think when they hear that I have "got religion." I imagine trying to explain the rather surprising shift from a lifetime of atheism to a belief in—what?

When I fell off the edge of the world after Terry's death in 2003, I experienced a raw terror that can still chill my very soul when I think of it. It wasn't just grief, although God knows that was hard enough; it was what's called, in griefspeak, "the shattering of the assumptive universe." I was in freefall through blackness; at times it felt as if my nose was being violently pushed into pure arbitrariness. The force pushing the back of my head snarled, "Nothing matters, nothing means anything, nothing is worth doing, or thinking, or caring about. The universe is chaotic, random, arbitrary." I saw the truth, and the truth was unbearable.

I remember talking on the phone with a friend who was trying to decide whether to go back and buy a blouse she had seen on sale. I felt a creepy sense of being cut off from everyone in the "normal" world, that there was an impenetrable scrim between me and other people. I absolutely could not imagine wanting a new blouse, on sale or otherwise.

Losing the desire to shop—now that's despair.

Ten days after Terry died, I flew to New Brunswick to stay with a friend at her cottage near Parlee Beach on the Northumberland

Strait. For most of the week the weather was cool and damp, the skies were grey, and that suited me just fine. I was in no mood for sunshine.

Terry loved the classical guitar repertoire, and in his last days I often played him Vivaldi's Guitar Concertos, even as he fell into unconsciousness. In New Brunswick I walked along the beach for hours each day, listening to Vivaldi, lost in my private world of pain.

One drizzly morning I walked out, glanced up and saw that there was no horizon line. The sea and the sky were one shimmering, opalescent grey, and the colour seemed strangely familiar. It was the exact shade of Terry's ashes as the late summer evening sunlight fell on them when our small group of friends and family scattered them in the ravine behind our house. It was as if Terry's spirit filled my entire field of vision, as if the whole world was made of pure dove-coloured light.

Then I saw, only about twenty feet in front of me, a heron, standing as they do, absolutely still. I don't know how long that bird and I stood there, in blessed communion. I felt the whole world was infused with the softest and loveliest spirit, a spirit that connected me, the heron, Terry, everyone I knew and loved, both living and dead, and beyond, every being, every blade of grass, every grain of sand on the beach. I knew that for the rest of my life, whenever I saw something quiet and peaceful and soft, that Terry would be there.

When Terry was dying of brain cancer, he wanted to find some kind of spiritual advisor. He had been a Discalced Carmelite monk for nine years, from his late teens to late twenties, but had broken with the church. Someone recommended a psychologist who specialized in treating patients with terminal diagnoses, but after seeing him once, Terry felt that this man had a prurient, vicarious interest in his, Terry's, impending death. We went to the chaplain's office at Princess Margaret Hospital, where Terry was being treated, to arrange a meeting with the woman chaplain there. All over the bookcases, the desk and the counter were dozens and dozens of little figurines of angels. I think we both gagged.

Then someone told Terry about another chaplain at the hospital, an openly gay Anglican priest. Terry went to see Douglas Graydon and asked me to go with him to see him again. Douglas had told him about being the only non-medical staff who would visit AIDS patients at St. Michael's Hospital. Eventually he became the chaplain at Casey House, the hospice for AIDS patients. In one year alone he conducted seventy-five funerals. This man knew how to walk people to the grave. Like Terry, he was modest and unassuming; he had a quiet, understated demeanour and a gentle wit. The first time I met him I had the strange but oddly convincing sense that he was a conduit, that he stood between me and the divine, or whatever I thought the divine might be at that time. "Oh," I thought, "I guess that's what priests are supposed to do."

Terry and I continued to see him, separately and together. A few months before Terry died, I encouraged him to spend some time with his two adult children, and booked him a ticket to Cuba for them to spend a week together. (We had been given a very specific prognosis: nine to twelve months. Terry lived exactly ten and a half months after the diagnosis.) Douglas came to the house to visit me. I was in a terrible state of indecision. I wanted to go to Big Sur, to the Esalen Institute, to take a workshop consisting of five hikes, each a day long, in the Ventana Mountains, while Terry was in Cuba.

"What if something happens and I'm not here?" I said to Douglas. We were day drinking wine in my living room. Douglas enjoyed his tipple.

"Of course you should go," he said. "You need it, and Terry needs you to have this respite."

"You're giving me your priestly imprimatur?"

"You have my Apostolic blessing."

On the second day's hike we came to a place where two rivers converged. I stood and watched the roiling waters. It occurred to me that when two rivers converge, just as when two people's lives converge, they can never be separated. Their molecules have mingled. If the river forks, each carries the other. I described this to Douglas when I got back.

"You had a religious experience," he said. "I'm jealous."

After Terry died I asked Douglas to officiate at his celebration of life. Then I saw him for grief counselling. But it wasn't enough. I wanted—needed—more of this funny, kind man.

When I returned from my trip to New Brunswick, I heard that Douglas had been hired as the priest-in-charge at St. Philip the Apostle Anglican Church on Caribou Road, near Bathurst and Lawrence. Fittingly, as I'm half Jewish, in an almost entirely Jewish neighbourhood. I started going to his services. If Doug had been a rabbi, I would have gone to a synagogue. I knew little and cared less about Anglicanism. Fortunately, the St. Philippians were an elderly but progressive bunch, and had done away with as much of the traditional liturgy as the Diocese would stomach. And then there were all those Trollope novels I had read, and all that Metaphysical poetry, in which the language of the Book of Common Prayer was embedded. I loved the cadences of the service.

A few parishioners had objected to the idea of a gay priest, and some had left. In response to this Douglas's partner Stephen would arrive at church and sit in the front pew, wearing tight black leather shorts. He sat beside me and guided me through the impossible to follow order of service, and once I'd learned the melodies of some of the hymns, he'd sing the harmonies. Each word of the hymns trembled with sacredness.

For a few years, I actually managed never to say the words Jesus or Christ out loud as we read the responses. Surely I couldn't become a Christian? For one thing, I imagined my Bubbeh and Zayde turning over in their graves. They were, by all accounts, not religious (none of their five sons, including my father, had a Bar Mitzvah) but they were Yiddish-speaking, cultural Jews. For another, I couldn't get past the collusion of the Church of England with the British Monarchy and the slave trade.

In most Christian churches, regardless of the denomination, only baptized Christians are allowed to take Communion. This was one of the many strictures St. Philips had done away with. To my astonishment, I found myself longing for "the cookies and milk" as a friend calls it. I wanted the body and the blood. One Sunday, trembling with nerves and anticipation, I went up and knelt at the altar rail and held out my hands as Douglas administered the sacrament. I felt like I had put my finger in a socket; a jolt of what I can only describe as divine energy ran through me. From that moment to this I have almost never missed a Sunday service or the chance to take Communion. Just before St. Philips was deconsecrated and torn down, I wanted to have one last ritual there. On Easter Sunday, 2010, I was baptized by Douglas. As I tilted my head back and received the holy water he sprinkled on my forehead, I was home.

Just like in any dysfunctional family, there is much to bemoan, but also much to love.

Even after getting a Master's degree in Theological Studies from Regis College, even after six or seven years of being a Spiritual Director, being a witness to many people on their spiritual path, I still have to put "Christian" in quotation marks. Some of the story I believe, and some I don't. Virgin birth? Loaves and fishes? Rising up from the dead? Yet year by year, the social gospel becomes ever more compelling. Feed the hungry, visit the prisoner, free those in bondage, suffer the little children. And year by year, the great archetypal story of death and resurrection sustains me. I'm surprised again and again, when hope returns with the green buds of spring, with the knowledge that everything dies, but all of nature lives. That, as Thomas Merton said, death doesn't happen at the end of life, it happens in the midst of life.

Living through the pandemic, the fast-approaching environmental apocalypse, the rise of fascism around the world, I've had my times of despair. What sentient being does not? In those times I return to glimpse the random arbitrariness and meaninglessness I experienced, what's glibly called an existential crisis, in the months after Terry's death. My "religious experiences" on Parlee Beach and in Big Sur didn't dispel it altogether; rather the vision of light and the heron co-existed with the dread. I found this haiku:

Broken and broken again on the sea
The moon so easily mends

Who can separate the black ocean from the dancing light of the moon? It is the light *and* the dark, the being broken *and* the being mended: that is God for me.

The Blue Heron—Theodore Goodridge Roberts

In a green place lanced through
With amber and gold and blue;
A place of water and weeds
And roses pinker than dawn,
And ranks of lush young reeds,
And grasses straightly withdrawn
From graven ripples of sands,
The still blue heron stands.

Smoke-blue he is, and grey
As embers of yesterday.
Still he is, as death;
Like stone, or shadow of stone,
Without a pulse or breath,
Motionless and alone
There in the lily stems;
But his eyes are alive like gems.

Still as a shadow; still
Grey feather and yellow bill:
Still as an image made
Of mist and smoke half hid
By windless sunshine and shade,
Save when a yellow lid
Slides and is gone like a breath;
Death-still—and still as death!

A BREAKUP LETTER

Dear Robin,

    I am writing in sadness to say my last goodbye to you. We've had a great run, and I'm so grateful to you for all the places you took us to see (over 50 countries!) and all the activities we've enjoyed together—baseball, running, skipping rope; and later, swimming, bicycling, and hiking in beautiful places all over the world. I especially want to thank you for the things we did the last few years, when I knew I was getting too old, tired and ache-y—for the yoga, the tai chi, the short walks with the dog, the aquapilates.

    I feel that I held up my end of the relationship very well, year after year, until I couldn't any longer. Everything hurts now, and as Leonard Cohen sang, "I'm ready my Lord."

    I know my replacement will be young and sleek, and will carry you through the last chapters of your life with ease. I am not jealous. (Maybe a little jealous.) I know you have learned that it is possible to have two great loves. So, it's not you, it's me. I can only support your decision, I can no longer hold up your body. I have loved our time together, times when we have jumped up in joy, and times when we have knelt down in suffering and prayer. Times when we bore down in childbirth, and times when we scattered the ashes of one we loved. Now someone else will take my place. I'm glad he will take you swimming and hiking again.

So farewell, may your last days be a blessing. May you feel the sunshine on your path, and the soft rain, and the sharp cold snow. May you in all seasons be serene and happy and no longer in the pain you've endured for years.

With much love,
Your Right Knee
May, 2017

GINGER COOKIES

I take a bite, frown. My friend Joss has made ginger cookies, and brought them over for a pandemic treat on the patio. She sees my expression and complains that there were about twenty steps, and six separate spices. A sophisticated recipe for ginger cookies is surely an oxymoron. They taste too complicated to be good. I get out my old friend Nancy's cookbook, a scribbler in which she wrote out by hand all her favourite recipes—cakes, cookies and "squares." She gave it to me for Christmas in 1968.

> ¾ c. short.
> 1 c. white sugar

(There are no instructions; Nancy assumed, rightly, that I knew the basics of making cookie dough).

I had been married two years, and was still only nineteen, when my father offered my husband the chance to run a business for him in Aylesford, Nova Scotia. It was a moribund peat moss bog operation. Henry had been learning the ropes from my father, the peat moss magnate of British Columbia, during summers between our years at the University of British Columbia.

In April of 1965 Henry and I drove across Canada, from Vancouver to Nova Scotia, following the spring as we travelled. The last leg of the trip was from New Brunswick to the Annapolis Valley. Approaching it from the south, we crested the hill (known, hilariously to us British Columbians, as the South Mountain), stopped and looked out at that peaceful landscape, just coming into the first pale green of spring.

When I was a child, I had four favourite jigsaw puzzles (which I've never been able to find again), one for each season, based on paintings by Grandma Moses or someone like her. The Annapolis Valley, as I gazed over it, reminded me of the Spring puzzle from that series—a fairy-tale landscape, lost in time. It felt strangely familiar, scaled to fit me, not like the high drama of the B.C. coastline, with its ever-changing mountains, clouds, and seascapes. This was a vista to comfort. I felt like I'd come home.

Before long we found an apartment in Berwick and I, still a teenager, and halfway to a university degree, became a housewife. There was a knock at the door, and the woman from across the street presented me with a homemade cake to welcome us to the neighbourhood. Frances and I became instant friends. The first time I crossed the street to visit her and her three daughters (six-year-old Heather, the youngest, was the giggliest child I ever met), there was a hardcover book prominently displayed on a side table in her parlour. It was called *The Cruelest Month*. That's April, I said. "Now, how did you know that?" Frances asked, astounded. Well, it's a line from a poem by T.S. Eliot, I said. She opened the frontispiece to show me the attribution. It was the second book by her cousin, Ernest Buckler, who had written the iconic Canadian novel *The Mountain and the Valley*. "Well, aren't you just the most clever person," she exclaimed, delighted to know someone who knew about April. Her genuine pleasure was a little thrill, a little shock. Being smart was never a social cachet where I came from, in the era in which I had come of age.

¼ c. molasses
1 egg

Frances and her cohort—namely the six other wives and mothers who lived on our street in Berwick (population around a thousand at that time), met every morning at ten for coffee at one or another of their houses. They would already have long been up, making hearty breakfasts, sending husbands to work and children to school, peeling the potatoes and carrots for "dinner," the main meal of the day, eaten at noon. They knew every tiny detail of the lives around them and gossiped and laughed with a gusto that I felt drawn into with a gleefulness to match theirs. How I loved those women! And how they loved me, this awkward, childless young egghead, learning how to bake and cook from them.

I only longed for one thing, which was to be invited to join the Wednesday evening sewing circle. This was reserved for Berwick's elite, and I had to wait several weeks before being asked to join. Perhaps because it was held in the evening, the gossip, as we embroidered pillow cases, aprons and tea towels, knitted bonnets for newborns and scarves for husbands, was a little racier, the laughter a little louder and more robust.

In the fall, I reluctantly left the morning coffee meetings, and the Wednesday evening sewing circle, to renew my studies again, this time at Dalhousie University. Frances told me that her sister, Nancy, lived in Halifax, and that she would arrange for us to stay with her until we found a place to live. We discovered, fortuitously, there was an apartment right across the street from Nancy, her husband and her two children. And Nancy and I, like Frances and I the previous spring, also became instant friends. The symmetry of living across the street from each of these two sisters seemed fated.

> *2 c. flour*
> *¼ t. salt*
> *2 t. soda*

A shy, awkward, and painfully self-conscious young woman, I came into my own at Dalhousie University. I started writing for the *Dalhousie Gazette*, and quickly got promoted to News Editor. I acted in all the campus productions, and became notorious for my role as Mrs. Barker in Edward Albee's absurdist play, *The American Dream*.

"Are you sure you're comfortable?" asks my friend Linda (Features Editor for the *Dalhousie Gazette*), in her role as Mommy. "Would you like to take off your dress?" "Thank you, I don't mind if I do," says Mrs. Barker. And off comes the dress, to reveal a very short red slip with lace around the bust and hem. This caused quite a stir in Halifax (where it was rumoured a student had been suspended the year before for playing tennis on a Sunday), and my scandalous act was the subject of an hour-long call-in radio program. Outraged citizens voiced their disgust. Other citizens lined up for tickets.

Through it all was Nancy, having us over for supper (remember, dinner was at noon), laughing at my exploits, cheering me on. Every Wednesday she cleaned the house from top to bottom. Baked every Saturday. Sunday nights she polished her husband's and her children's shoes. Every night, after she made all three of their lunches, she and Ern had coffee and some of her baked treats. The very goodies she had written out the recipes for, when I came back to visit for Christmas the year after I graduated.

I didn't see much of Frances and Nancy over the years. We sent Christmas cards and letters; they continued to follow my path through life with enormous affection and amusement. When my daughter was fourteen, I wanted her to experience the Maritimes, so we flew to Moncton from Toronto, and drove from there to Berwick. I wanted her to see the Valley as I had first seen it. Of course Frances made a cake, and told my daughter endless funny stories about her mother. Stories polished in the retellings to a smooth patina. The time I persuaded Frances and Nancy to go to a lecture with me at Acadia University. I sat and knitted; they sat and were bored. I asked a question. "She didn't drop a stitch, and the lecturer had to admit he didn't know the answer. And she just kept on knitting!" The most notorious of all stories, the time Henry and I invited the whole neighbourhood to a pig roast in our backyard. Everyone showed up at 6. "Henry, where's the pig?" Frances asked. The pig was still walking. Henry, who had apprenticed as a butcher in Germany, went and slaughtered the pig, cut it up and roasted it, and we ate at around 10 pm. We never did live that one down.

1 t. cinnamon
1 t. cloves
1 t. ginger

I took my daughter to Halifax and we had lunch with Nancy and Ern, so proud to show us the newly revitalized waterfront. More hilarious stories—the time Nancy had a little gathering after the opening night of *The American Dream*, and I invited my English professor (on whom I had a torrid, undeclared crush). Ern asked if he could hang up his coat, and the professor handed him a cape. Ern didn't know what to do with it. "A cape! For a man! Who ever heard of such a thing?"

I told Nancy then how much she and Frances had meant to me, how I thrived and blossomed in the light of their acceptance of me, in their housewifery and motherhood. A few days later, driving to the airport, my daughter said, quite out of the blue, "You know, in the Jewish religion, the highest good you can do is to give someone something without them knowing it, and that's what Frances and Nancy did for you." "Yes," I said, "I know. It's called a *mitzvah*."

Nova Scotia, in the person of these kind, generous and funny women, shaped my sense of who I am, gave me unconditional love and acceptance I'd never known before, and rarely have known since.

Roll in balls and dip in white sugar.
Bake 375

The scribbler is torn and tattered and stained with the residue of eggs, sugar, and butter. I made Nancy's ginger cookies and shared them among friends and neighbours. This is *le vrai* ginger cookie recipe—the taste of everything comforting, home-y, familiar. Everyone loved them.

BRIAN SHEIN AND ME: IN MEMORIAM

My friend Barbara gave me an antique hand-coloured photograph, maybe 5" × 7", of babies in a cabbage patch. She found the perfect frame for it, a patina-ed brass in a swirly shape. It had pride of place in the upstairs hall on a small oak bureau. It pleased me every time I walked past it.

> I can't remember
> I can't remember
> I can't remember
> I don't want to remember

In the mid-seventies, I was a teaching assistant for a course in Canadian Studies at York University. I led the module on Canadian Literature, but we each also had to teach every other subject in the course—history, politics, and art. I read a lot and learned a lot that year. There was a section in the history part of the course on Indigenous Studies. This was almost fifty years ago; we knew little of what we know today. Most of the literature (all by whites) was about the pros and cons of assimilation. I found it mystifying and dreary.

But one day one of the course directors brought in a half-hour documentary for us to watch. It was called *Potlatch: A Strict Law Bids Us Dance*. It told the story of the Kwakiutl (as they were called then) in Alert Bay holding elaborate potlatch rituals, with feasting, dancing, singing, and gift-giving. The greatest esteem came to the one who gave away the most—the ultimate antithesis of capitalism. The Department of Indian Affairs, under the celebrated Canadian poet, Duncan Campbell Scott, outlawed the potlatch, and they were raided. People were sent to jail, their offenses listed as singing, or dancing. "A strict law bids us dance," was a quote from one of the defendants at their trial. Ceremonial masks were taken—stolen—and wound up in museums and private collections, including that of Duncan Campbell Scott. The movie was made, with the Kwakiutl anthropologist Gloria Webster, as both a protest and an activist tool to lobby for the return of the sacred artifacts to Alert Bay. I was moved and impressed by the cogency, the wit, the ardent call to action, and the cinematography. I promised myself if I ever met either of the two writers of the film—Dennis Wheeler or Brian Shein—I would marry him.

The following summer, after a Saturday matinee at some experimental downtown theatre, a group of us, some known, some new, went for supper at Sai Woo, the now defunct go-to Chinese restaurant in Toronto. My friend, the director and actor Cheryl Cashman, introduced me around, saying, "Oh, Robin, I want you to meet Brian. He made a movie about the potlatch." I stood completely still, feeling my face go hot. My friend Lesley was already chatting him up with a glint in her eye, but she didn't have a whisper of a chance. He was mine. It was fate.

Brian at that time was literally a starving writer (he once told me he hadn't eaten for three days—I marched him down to the welfare office), writing for the *National Lampoon* in its heyday and other more obscure publications that paid peanuts or nothing. The first time he came to my house I said, "You're welcome to snoop around if you like." This offer surprised him and endeared me to him. Our mutual friend Cheryl was also more or less starving, and as I had a house with two extra bedrooms, and occasional infusions of cash from my father to keep us all in groceries, they moved in with me.

When I told my mother about him, on one of her drunken phone calls to me (8 am Toronto time, 5 am Vancouver all-night-drinking time), she was unimpressed with his accomplishments. "How tall is he?" she asked. "Is he taller than you?" "No, he's quite short," I said. "Ah ha! So you can dominate him!" My sister was kinder. "I've met someone, he's a humourist, he writes for the *National Lampoon*." "Wow, great score, Robin!" she said.

My nickname for him was Mouse, and we started collecting tiny figurines of mice. Once when I came back home after a weekend at a friend's cottage, he had left me a "scene" on the kitchen table (the round oak table I have to this day), made of pieces of mirror for lakes, tea cups with rose petals, tiny mice and tiny paper boats. His courtship was enchanted and enchanting. We were like two children creating a magic world only we inhabited. He invented a character based on me as a child, called Binky Bell, World's Greatest Communist, and left notes to me addressed to Bink, W.G.C. I still have the hilarious stories he wrote about her adventures saving children from cruel sweatshop managers.

He left this parody of Robert Browning on the washing machine one day after he fixed it for me when I was out teaching:

Andrea Del Smarto

What's that, my lass? Washer's on fritz? Pooped out?
Stuck i' mid-cycle, say you? Piffle, Bink!
Th' merest trifle when home-handyman's about.
There's my last triumph perched above the sink—
That madd'ning faucet—hang it!—with its drip.
"Quick! Hand me th' crescent wrench!" (Do you recall?)
Tap's fixed i' jiffy! Huzza!" Thus we nip
Irks i' th' bud. Now—laundry's kaput? Bulks small
Of scope as sense in nudnik's noggin. Pah!
Washing's my *forte*. I twist and turn again
Dials on th' machine—hey, presto!—*et voila*—
Smooth as the Pope's conscience—wash, rinse, spin, drain!
Eh? Can't be done? Look you—clothes clean and dry
Proof's pudding's cooked and served. Never say die!
    —Robert Mouseling

We called each other Susan, in homage to Jessica and Nancy Mitford, the sisters who also called each other Susan. One of us might leave a note—"Dear Susan, I'm off to a rehearsal/to teach/to an editorial meeting. There's eggs and milk in the fridge. Love, Susan."

I had a very clear career path marked out as an academic. I planned to start a Cultural Studies Institute, which would examine all aspects of Canadian culture from a Marxist perspective. I would be its Director. An obstacle to this vision presented itself—I wasn't able to get a job at any university in Canada after I got my PhD. There was effectively a job freeze going on. (This was in the mid-seventies.) Also I found out through an acquaintance on a hiring committee that my thesis supervisor, with whom I thought I had an excellent relationship, had written a letter of recommendation that said I was an outspoken activist, and I'd be a thorn in the side of any department that hired me. So no one did.

After three degrees in English Literature, I thought I knew a thing or two about the canon, but I learned more in six months of talking about fiction, prose, and poetry with Brian than I had in six years. I didn't realize it at the time, but he was teaching me how to be an artist, how to take the creative life seriously; indeed, take it as a matter of life and death. How to throw out the first paragraph, how to appreciate the economy, the beauty, the wit of great writing and great art. We took the train to Windsor in a snow storm, and the ferry across the river to Detroit, to see a retrospective of Matisse. "Look at his line," Brian said. "Just look at that line!" I never saw art in the same way again. I was learning to look at art, to read literature, as an artist rather than a critic.

I spent years learning to think and write like male academics. Now I would have to unlearn, drill down through the layers of academese and Marxist theory to find the creative lava that burned deep within me. From being known in academic and Marxist circles as having a "heavy head," and being a "big brain," I had to learn how to be a child again, to play, to honour my imagination.

The first thing I did was write a stage adaptation of Lucy Maud Montgomery's children's book *Magic for Marigold*. I persuaded my friend Kent Biggar to compose music to my lyrics, and I directed a production of it with an amateur group called The Saint Joan of Arc Players. It was probably a disaster; certainly the adjudicator for the Sears Festival, the annual festival of amateur theatre, thought so. But the Prince Edward Island poet Milton Acorn came to see it and told me: "Never let anyone tell you otherwise, you captured something few people have, about the nature of the Island. Lucy Maud would be proud of you."

And Brian wrote this poem for me for the opening night. At that time I had started calling myself Robin Belitsky Endres. (My father's name was Belitsky before he assimilated and changed it to Bell, the surname I grew up with. When I finally did feel like an artist, and not a fraud, I gave up all these various patriarchal surnames and legally changed my surname to Pacific.)

THE LOVER SALUTES HIS LADY
AS SHE PREPARES TO TREAD THE BOARDS

(Composed after a Brief Sojourn
In the Era of the Primitive Accumulation)

R obin whose heart to Stardom doth aspire,
O 'ertopping chill Parnassus' lofty slope,
B urning with Thespia's many-coloured fire,
I lluminating all with brilliant scope—
N ever forget that Genius must be bold,
B lazoning Truth across the crest of Art.
B eware Canuck'ry with its accents cold
E xcept to spark the passions of its Heart.
L et everything you are be what we see.
I nspire us with your sorrows and your joys
T o dare the heights, shine starlike and be free.
S peak up, speak out. We need to hear your voice.
K now, Robin, I remain until the end
Y our happy comrade and devoted friend.
    —July 7, 1978

He had some memorable one-liners, still quoted by me and his friends. He called Sai Woo, the Chinese restaurant where we met, and which was a mecca for Toronto Jews, "the Sino Sinai Poison Palace." Once when we were talking about living together, I said it's hard when you have to put up with the other person's disgusting personal habits. I was prone to biting my toenails. "How do you think I feel," he said, "walking into the bedroom and seeing your lips festooned with pedal garnishes?"

During the run of *Magic for Marigold*, we were both astonished when, as the old expression has it, I fell pregnant. "You're both children," my sister said. "You're living in a children's pretend world. How will you ever look after a baby, raise a child?"

We bought a big basket for the baby to sleep in, found an old butter box and lined it with pretty wallpaper. On one of his trips to New York, to work for the *National Lampoon*, Brian bought a darling little yellow baby dress, cotton-knit, with tiny flowers all over it. At Saks Fifth Avenue.

Our daughter was born at home, after a seven-hour labour, short for a first birth. My sister was right. The existence of an actual baby exploded our fantasies of babies and children, written about by Brian and drawn by me. Suddenly there were endless tasks, laundry, grocery shopping, cooking. Changing diapers, feeding the baby, walking with her for hours in the night in the futile hope that she would stop crying. Always hyper-sensitive to noise, I felt like her screams were inside my head. She woke every two hours through the night. I had never babysat or even looked after a friend's baby. We were both completely ignorant. Brian of course was praised to the moon for helping to take care of her. "You'd think the world shifted on its axis because a man changed a diaper," I said to his mother. I was always afraid something bad would happen to her, always on high alert. I had repeated dreams where I was supposed to be looking after a baby and I would forget about her, and frantically search for her. In other nightmares she would turn into a doll, and I wouldn't be able to turn her back into a live baby.

In the midst of all the chaos, nonetheless, was overpowering love, for her and for each other. "Look, she lifted her head, just when they said she would, at three months!" We almost fainted, this made us so happy.

When the baby was six months old, I was doing an "Artist in the Schools" project at a high school in Orangeville, teaching improvisation and scene writing. I got a painful infection in my eye, and had to go home in the middle of the day. Brian was there with the baby. We put her on a blanket on the living room rug and lit a fire in the fireplace. I lay on the couch, my feet on Brian's lap. Since I had to keep my painful eye closed, he read aloud to me the entirety of Pablo Neruda's book-length poem, *The Heights of Macchu Picchu*. When he got to the end I was weeping. "What's the matter?" Brian asked. "It's just that the language is so beautiful." In that moment, I think each of us felt completely seen. It was one of the most intimate times we ever had.

I'm not sure when, or how, it all went bad. I'm not sure whether I can't remember because I don't want to remember.

We had both been hospitalized at points in our lives for mental illness, and in hindsight, I think sleep deprivation exacerbated some features of our respective manias. Brian had a kind of Tourette's—he would get angry about something, and then it was as if he was possessed. He shook up the milk in a milk bottle and sprayed it all over the kitchen table. He went on bizarre paranoid rants, often accusing me of being an agent of the KGB (the obverse of Binky Bell, World's Greatest Communist). For my part, I turned into my mother, mocking, and belittling him. I became anhedonic, couldn't bear the thought of having sex with him.

There are no words for how ashamed I feel, forty years later, and thirty-three years after his death, for how cruel I was to him, how angry, how jealous of his work. It is the great regret of my life, and no matter how hard I have tried, down the years, to forgive myself, I think I will carry that regret all the rest of my days.

One night, in one of his rages, he lifted up the picture of the little babies in the cabbage patch and smashed it on the floor. Glass flew everywhere. He threw it so hard that the metal frame broke. It was one in the morning. I took the child from her bed, called a taxi, woke up my friend Lesley, and went to stay with her.

A few weeks later, Brian walked out, and never came back. I was sad, angry, and lonely. He got an apartment in the neighbourhood and started having our child with him a few days a week.

By all reports, he was doing just fine. He had a large circle of friends to support him in his Twelve Step program. A poet "friend" —ostensibly *my friend*, ostensibly a *feminist*—had him over for dinner every Friday night, and there was always a single, interesting, attractive woman she'd invited for him to meet.

We still fought. The school sent home a notice on one of the days he picked her up, about a little recital the children were having. He didn't tell me about it and took a "date" to see it. I was incensed, not least because I thought the teachers would think I didn't care enough to come. I called. "You little shit, why didn't you tell me? How do you think I felt? How do you think that looked for me?" His voice was calm, rational. "The recital was on one of my days, Robin, so of course you couldn't come to it. You're overreacting." "Overreacting? How dare you!" and so on. The truth is, by this point I knew, half consciously, precisely the triggers that would send him into one of his rage-possessed outbursts, and then I could play the victim. Toxic is a word that hardly describes this dynamic. How did we devolve from our sweet, childlike romance, full of poetry, art, and music, to this? How did our best selves become our worst?

I wrote him a letter. I told him that I didn't think I knew what love is, or how it feels. That there had been no love in my family. That I was going on a spiritual quest to find out what it is, how to recognize it.

That quest took me to the Esalen Institute in Big Sur, California. After a few week-long workshops, I felt a profound need to spend more time there. I felt if I had six months, I could straighten myself out, make sense of my rages, my extreme anxieties, my doubts, my need to find some kind of spiritual path. I could learn how to be a mother.

At first I wanted to leave my daughter, now seven, with Brian, but he refused, saying he had to work. He was just beginning to get a stable income and career going, working as a staff writer for

Toronto Life magazine. I offered to pay for a housekeeper but he refused that as well. I knew someone who had a sister who was raising her children on a farm outside the city. I thought she might be happy there. In retrospect I think that neither of us was mentally stable enough to take care of her, and we blamed each other. Then my sister came to Toronto. We were sitting on bar stools at the Queen Mother on Queen Street, waiting for a table. She turned to me and said: "Robin, you have to take her with you. You can't leave her with anyone else, especially strangers. I'm telling you, you have no choice."

So I had my six months, struggling to work in the organic garden as a single mother. Perhaps inevitably, I became involved with a man and wanted to spend longer and longer amounts of time there. Brian was incensed. He wanted to be with his daughter. Understandably. He didn't want me to take her to Big Sur, ever, and was trying to find legal ways to stop me. We became embroiled in a vicious custody dispute, in the midst of which he was diagnosed with adenocarcinoma—a kind of systemic cancer that attacks all the organs at once. Six weeks later he was dead.

As I sit writing this, in the middle of the pandemic, on a cold February day, the wind is keening and whining around the back door. Brian died at what now seems such a young age, forty-one, in 1986, and I can still feel the icy fist of grief tighten around my heart. In spite of how things turned out, I miss him, his humour, his genius, his kindness. Our daughter lost her father at eight, a lifelong trauma. And Canada lost a writer who, I'm certain, would have made a major, significant contribution to the literary life of this country.

I believe that had he lived, we would have found our way out of the morass of bitterness and recrimination we had both fallen into. We would have gotten on our feet as artists; he would have figured out how to make a living; we would have healed some of the wounds of our respective childhoods. We would have become friends and good parents, both of us. Fate didn't give us that second chance. At heart he was a gentle man, a man of deep sensitivity and compassion. He died *in media res*. His life was unresolved. We were unresolved. His death is still, over thirty years later, the greatest tragedy of my life.

SAND

We all just want to be in front of the camera, to be filmed for posterity, to be seen, to be valued. Our fifteen minutes. Instead we end up as bones or ashes, mysterious and a little boring. Not even of interest to ourselves. Grains of sand. Anonymous. Perhaps we each, should we be blessed with grandchildren, or have friends' grandchildren who know us, have fifty years to survive in the memories of the living. Then pouf! All gone! Fifty years, an eyeblink in eternity. So what legacy do we leave, do we yearn for, what shadow of immortality can we dream of, if all we are, all we can hope to be, is an insignificant speck of dust? Of sand? None. Nothing.

But ... suppose each grain of sand on this earth is the soul of someone who has once lived, and each grain of sand is an entire universe when its molecular structure is seen in a microscope. And each grain of sand is singular, unique. Such is the miracle of individual consciousness: mysterious, monumental, eternal. And the eye of God the camera recording every soul, every moment, every instance of pain, triumph, failure, and love.

I KNOW WHAT I LIKE

Union Station is the southernmost stop and the end point of Toronto's subway system. I call it the Horn of Africa, or sometimes, Antarctica. I like to go there for the art on its walls, large gestural drawings encased in glass. The drawings are of people on the subway, each seemingly lost in thought. Some appear to be sad. Many riders dislike these drawings, and complain about them, saying they are depressing. But to me they are a multitude of solitudes, conveying the experience of riding the subway, or perhaps of urban life in general. Some enlightened art bureaucrat must have fought for them, and I am grateful to this person. It's not easy to advocate for good art and win.

Much of the art I see in galleries is so pale, so little, so insignificant, I can hardly stand to go any more. There is so little that is expansive, risk taking, bold. There is so much wanking. "All that retinal art," Marcel Duchamp said. For art to be art, it has to matter. A lot.

I make no claim for my own work. I'm of the Jean Rhys school of art theory. I once read a catalogue essay about Willem de Kooning. (A painter I like very much, incidentally.) The writer (male) said that de Kooning had singlehandedly changed the course of the river of modern painting. Speaking of wanking. Shortly after I read that the novelist Jean Rhys said she wanted to be a drop of water in the immense lake of literature. So that's what I've aspired to. A drop in the lake of art.

Many, many thousands of trees have surrendered their lives for our paper, and many, many children have died mining the cobalt for the batteries in our devices, so that many, many people can write articles, usually obscure, about art theory. What is art? What is an artist? What is good versus bad art? Abstract art in particular is a language-generating medium; art itself is a meaning-making machine. It seems the less content in the work, the less representation, the more words are needed to talk about it. But from Aristotle down to the present, it remains a mystery. A friend claims that Carl Jung's theories are so compelling that they encompass art. I beg to differ. Nothing encompasses art. It cannot be contained, by any system of thought or philosophy or knowledge. It is its own is-ness.

When I first started to learn to draw and paint, I thought that no work of visual art could ever move me the way I had been moved in my years of reading the canon of English literature. No painting could make me feel the agony of a naked King Lear as his mind shatters in the storm on the heath. No painting could convey the startling modernity, simplicity, and profundity of the ending of that play:

> The weight of this sad time we must obey,
> Speak what we feel, not what we ought to say.

Words I used on the program for my late husband's memorial.

Then one day I came upon one of Rembrandt's self-portraits in the Frick gallery in New York, one of the ones he painted when he was old. I felt like I was stabbed in some hidden part of my soul. And I also felt connected to the man in the painting and the man who painted it. I had to eat my words about language being more powerful than images. By what magic, by what alchemy, can pigments on canvas say so much, mean so much, change me so much?

"What's Hecuba to him, or he to Hecuba, that he should weep for her?" Hamlet says in the play within the play, asking the unanswerable question of how art does what it does.

Of course, some will argue that the role of art is not to evoke emotion, and whole schools of work, such as Conceptual Art and Minimalism (some of which I also like very much) eschew feeling in favour of pure idea or pure form. I'll take that too. In fact, I'll take all of it. When I see or read something I love, something that connects me, something that changes me, I always say a little mantra to myself: *I'm glad I gave my life to art.*

BLACK-EYED DOROTHY

My parents went to an event at the golf course, leaving me home alone. I was about fifteen.

Bored and a little lonely, I went to sleep. In the middle of the night, they burst into my bedroom and turned on the light. My mother had red welts on her face and arm, and the beginning of a black eye.

"You see what your father did to me?" she said.

"You see what your mother made me do?" my father said.

When they left, I snuck into the kitchen and called my newly married sister. "Oh well Robin," she said. "Think of it this way: one day you'll be able to write about it."

ONE STROKE AND YOU'RE OUT

I remember my mother and her friend Sylvia laughing and laughing together. Sylvia had bright red hair. She was *zaftig*, and waltzed into our house with all sails unfurled. She had a husband, Harold, who was as bland and pale as she was vivacious. Like my mother, she was a fifties housewife with three children. Then Sylvia had some kind of breakdown, it was all very hush hush, and she was sent to Essondale.

Essondale! That's where crazy people were sent to be locked up. If you were a child, being threatened with a sojourn in Essondale could always result in good behaviour, at least for a while. Sylvia was subjected to electroshock therapy and given sodium pentathol, "truth serum." I overheard my mother on the phone telling another friend in a low, conspiratorial voice: "They take you right back to when we were apes, and then through all ages of human history, and then they jolt you with electricity."

Sylvia's breakdown had a deep effect on my mother. An atheist for as long as I remembered, she suddenly took up an interest in reincarnation, reading late into the night, sleeping until noon, and telling us about her discoveries at the dinner table. She also became fascinated with psychiatry and decided, to everyone's astonishment, that she wanted to become a psychiatrist.

She already had a Bachelor of Arts and loved to tell the story of how her father bitterly fought her desire to get an education. My grandfather believed women's place was in the home and schooling beyond high school was a sin. One summer my mother came home with her earnings, in cash, from waitressing at a resort. Her father stole the money. Because she couldn't afford bus fare, she walked to UBC from the West End of Vancouver that whole year.

Now, in her mid-forties, she applied to medical school and was accepted. In Vancouver in the 1950s, this would have been considered outlandish, bizarre even. But she was determined. She wanted to understand how the mind works, how the unconscious is structured.

Sarcasm was the lingua franca of the Bell household. The barbs were witty, but you were always pulling them out of your side. The poet Milton Acorn perfectly sums up my experience: *I was born into an ambush*. There was no *esprit de l'escalier*; if you didn't think of a quick retort you were symbolically kicked down the stairs, your psyche bleeding out on the floor. The Greek root of the word sarcasm means "the tearing of the flesh."

When I was around six or seven I decided to write a novel. The first chapter ended with the line: "She could hardly wait for next week." The second chapter began: "It was next week now!"

When I shyly showed it to my two older siblings they couldn't stop laughing. "It's next week now!" they chanted. If anyone asked what time it was, someone would always shout: "It's next week now!" I joined in the fun, and I never tried to write a story again. Eventually I too became skilled at the witty retort, a habit I still occasionally lapse into. I'll say something teasing to my partner, unaware of the sharp little stiletto knife buried underneath it, and I'm surprised to see the hurt, puzzled look in his eyes. Then the gelatin of remorse seeps into me. Around the Bell family dinner table of my youth, apologies were never offered. I still have trouble saying a simple "I'm sorry."

One Sunday, during a typical dinner, my brother was rocking back and forth on his chair (*Johnnie, stop rocking, you'll break the chair*); I was chewing my bubble gum as I ate my dinner (*Robin, get rid of that gum*); and my sister was daydreaming, staring off into space (*Caroline, pay attention*). My mother threw down her knife and fork with a loud clatter. She looked down the table at all of us. "Yup," she said. "That's what I got out of life, three squares and a flop!"

I wasn't able to deconstruct this wordplay until I was an adult. In the dirty thirties, the expression meant three square meals and a place to sleep, but of course she meant we three children, the squares, and my father, the flop. It was another brilliant witticism with a bitter aftertaste.

One day in Grade Seven I came in from school to discover no one was at home.

This seemed odd. I wandered around wondering where everyone was. In the bathroom I saw my mother's bloody nightgown lying in the bathtub. When my father finally came home, he told me my mother had had a stroke, and surgeons were going to operate on her brain the next day. *Arteriosclerosis* was a new word. A blood vessel had hardened and then burst in her brain. She was forty-four years old.

Two days later he took me to the hospital to see her. My Auntie Katie and my Aunt Marion were there. My mother's head was shaved. A long line of black and spiky stitches ran from one ear up and across her bare skull and down to the other ear. They looked angry, like barbed wire. She was babbling incoherently.

When I saw her, she terrified and repelled me and I ran out into the waiting room and into the arms of Auntie Katie, who held me as I cried. I had an odd sensation it wasn't really me crying, that I was putting on an act.

My mother was the first patient in Vancouver to undergo a new technique called "polar bear surgery." Her body temperature was lowered so that the lengthy surgery could take place without her dying. My father told me this dispassionately, as if polar bear surgery was the most important and interesting part of the story.

I've wondered my whole life if saving my mother's life was more a curse than a blessing.

Katie stayed with us while my mother was recuperating, such as it was, in the hospital, and stayed on for a couple of weeks after my mother came home. By now she could talk, although her words were still sometimes slurred, and she had bizarre behaviours: she could write a letter but was unable to read it back. One day, thinking she was lighting a cigarette, she put a match in her mouth and tried to light it with another match. Fortunately, Katie happened to walk into her bedroom and prevented what would almost certainly have been a fire.

And so ended the dream of medical school.

One day my Auntie Katie and I were roughhousing on the bed. "You know," she said, "it might be time for you to start using a deodorant."

I jumped up. It was as if someone had taken a knife and split me in two. I instantly loathed the sweaty, ugly body that had betrayed me in such a disgusting way. I began taking very long, very hot showers. As I scrubbed my arms and legs I was sure I could see dirt coming out of my pores. The harder I scrubbed, the more dirt came out, and no matter how hard I tried, I couldn't get clean.

A few weeks after my mother came home, and after Auntie Katie had returned to her home, my father walked out. He left my sister enough money to quit her summer job and stay home to look after my mother, me, and the house. My cute and popular older brother, now in his first year at UBC, moved into his frat house. Around three months later, my father came back. He just walked in, no explanation given.

By this time my mother had recovered enough for the fighting and the drinking, which had been the soundscape to our household, to resume. My father, a big man, was a heavy drinker, but he could take it or leave it. My mother, on the other hand, was on the road to the alcoholism that would eventually kill her.

My mother's rage fuelled her drinking, and her drinking in turn fuelled her rage. One by one her friends stopped coming to see her. My father went on more and longer "business trips"; came back for a while after she kicked him and me out; but eventually left her for good. Still, when she wasn't drinking they were on friendly terms and took many trips together.

As a young child, before I started school, I had very curly long blonde hair, and it was my mother's great ambition to turn it into ringlets. To this end, she rolled it up in sections in the orange papers which wrapped the Mandarin oranges we bought at the Chinese grocer. Nothing could induce a full-blown tantrum more than the orange paper proposition. Tantrums usually worked with my father but were more hit and miss with my mother. My earliest memories are of her pulling and twisting my hair, of my wanting more than anything for her to get her hands off me. I don't recall ever being hugged or cuddled by my mother, although I'm sure this must have happened. All I remember is not wanting her to touch me, ever.

As a teenager, I was trapped, shut down, and locked in an eternal power struggle with my mother. I always felt the same sense that she was grabbing me, pulling on my clothes. (*This skirt is too short! You're not leaving the house dressed like that!*) I was repelled by her touch and by the smell of alcohol. I never experienced tenderness or kindness from her. As a bright and talented woman, trapped and unwell (indeed, brain damaged), she must have hated my youth and my freedom.

My mother's story is the story of a whole generation of middle class women coerced into believing the road to happiness lay in domestic servitude, what the British Marxist Maurice Dobb called "the last peasant of capitalism."

My mother lived in the wrong time and was married to the wrong man. She was born with the wrong brain, a brain that exploded inside her skull, maimed her, and killed her thirty years before the rest of her died.

And maybe she had the wrong daughter. Perhaps she would have been happier with a more compliant girl, not someone who was as angry, headstrong, and stubborn as she. Instead, she got me, a daughter who did not, would not, could not love her. In her sad, blighted life, this was perhaps the greatest of all her sorrows.

POSTSCRIPT

What became of Sylvia, my mother's happy demented friend? Was she cured of her schizophrenia? I remember spending time at a cottage with Sylvia and her three children: Cindy, a year or two older than me, managed to be moody and phlegmatic at the same time; Jimmy, the boy, was called "slow" to his face, and "retarded" behind his back; Layla, the youngest, was a happy, carefree child and for a six-year-old, a good swimmer. All three had bright red hair, like their mother's. Harold wasn't there, or if he was, no one noticed.

Cindy and Layla and I spent hours at the dock, jumping into the lake, swimming as far away as we dared, swimming back, climbing up the ladder to the deck, jumping in again. Jimmy mostly stood on the end of the dock, his sunburn getting pinker and pinker. He had grown tall and plump; he didn't speak but communicated in grunts only his mother seemed to understand.

One day after breakfast, Sylvia announced she was going to give Jimmy a spanking. He had done nothing wrong as far as I could tell, but she insisted that he needed disciplining, and that sparing the rod would spoil the child. Sylvia had become quite religious after her breakdown and liked to quote scripture.

"Yes," she said, "before this day is over, I'm going to give Jimmy a spanking for his own good. Spare the rod! Spoil the child!"

Cindy couldn't meet my eyes. Layla kept splashing around in the lake. Jimmy stood at the end of the dock. Sylvia's harangue went on and on. On some strange impulse, I hauled back and with all my strength pushed Jimmy, that mountain of sunburned flesh, off the dock and into the lake.

A stupendous fuss ensued. Jimmy couldn't swim. Somehow Sylvia and Cindy pulled him on to the dock, dried him off. He was crying great gulping sobs. He was put to bed amidst much coddling, given hot chocolate. Sylvia berated me over and over.

"Don't you know he could have drowned? However could you do such a mean thing?"

Cindy's sorrow-filled eyes were worse than her mother's ranting. "I ought to call your mother and get her to take you home," Sylvia said. I knew it was an empty threat because my parents were travelling in some far-off country the Goulds had probably never even heard of. Why? Sylvia pressed me, why? I couldn't answer. I had no idea why. He was there, in his stupid, sunburned solidity. I was there. The lake called. I didn't know then why I did it and I don't know now. I do know that talk of rod sparing and child spoiling was forgotten for the rest of my vacation at the Gould's summer cottage.

JACKANAPES:
A PORTRAIT OF MY FATHER IN
TWENTY-TWO VIGNETTES

1. Fortune

My father passed down three rules for living:

1. Always turn off the light—it's not an eyelid, it doesn't shut by itself.
2. Never miss an opportunity to relieve yourself.
3. Always give money to a panhandler—tell yourself: "There but for fortune go I."

2. A Donkey, A Dog, A Dollar

I dreamed I was running in a race with hundreds of people, but I had to carry a baby donkey. The donkey snuggled in my arms, so silky soft, her breath like little puffs of clouds.

My father travelled a lot, always described as "being away on business," and he always brought me a stuffed animal when he returned. When I heard the front doorknob turning I hurtled down the hallway, yelling: "What did you bring me? Where's my stuffed animal?"

"Aren't you even glad to see me?" he asked. "Could you maybe say: 'Hi Daddy, How was your trip?' Give me a hug?"

"Where. Is. It? Where. Is. It?" I chanted, and because my father existed to do my bidding, he produced it. The stuffed animal that became the most loved was a dog whose long ears had insides that were soft and silky, just like the donkey in my dream. I arranged it carefully on my bed among the dozens lined up least to most favourite. He was quite floppy, so he was the one I pulled under the covers to sleep with, because he could mould himself to my body.

Once when my father was sleeping on the couch after dinner, I told my friend Libby, I could get him to give me a dollar. I shook his shoulder. "Daddy, I need a dollar, right now!" He reached in his pocket, gave me a dollar bill, and went right back to sleep.

3. Playing Favourites

I thoroughly enjoyed my status as a spoiled little princess, even if it meant my brother and sister routinely bullied me for it. I intuited I was the repository of my father's emotional life—that it was me (and not my eternally raging mother) to whom he looked for solace. I curled up under my father's arm for hours on the couch to read or watch TV. I'm sure, in this cozy nest, my smugness was insufferable to the rest of the family, including, of course, my mother. I knew he could refuse me nothing, and this gave me a delightful sense of power.

"I love all you kids," my father was fond of saying. "But you're my favourite, Robin. You're my little daddy's girl."

My mother frequently said, "I love all my children, but I have to say Johnnie is my favourite by far." Can these memories possibly be true? Did my parents ever actually say things like this? And how did Caroline, my older sister (nobody's favourite) feel? Liberated, perhaps.

4. Straight Outta Jeanne-Mance Street

He grew up in the Jewish ghetto in Montreal, Duddy Kravitz country. He changed his name from Isaiah Belitsky to Jack T. Bell. The T stood for Trouble. When he married my mother, a *shicksa*, his mother had an actual, not a metaphorical, heart attack. But my mother quickly won over her mother-in-law and her four sisters-in-law.

"I taught them how to roast a chicken, Robin—they only knew how to *boil* a chicken. After that, they loved me!" My *bubbeh* died when I was four, and I never met her, but I loved to hear stories about her from my mother.

"Your grandma always went to the open-air market on St. Laurent. She could bargain for ages and was always so proud when she got a good price. But one day she haggled and haggled with the butcher, and he just wouldn't give in. She swore in Yiddish, turned around and pulled up her skirt, right in front of him!"

5. Invisible

My father ate gefilte fish late at night alone in the kitchen. My siblings and I mocked him for this, shrieking with disgust and clutching our stomachs.

He took out a membership in the Vancouver Lawn Tennis Association, which barred membership to Jews, paying dues year after year, never making an appearance.

6. What Goes Up Must Come Down

After the war, on a veteran's grant, he bought up three peat moss bogs, on Lulu Island, now Richmond, B.C. At the time the land was almost worthless. He invented all the technology for harvesting, drying, compressing, and bagging peat moss, techniques still used today, and built those three peat bogs into a very successful business.

The CEO of a major international corporation, a man named Binnie Milner, came knocking at his door and hired him to make his company's own peat bogs profitable. This ushered in a period in the life of our family when my father travelled constantly, and we went on lavish trips and drove around in a fancy Ford convertible with (what were then unheard of) push-button windows. I was around nine years old at this time.

Then suddenly it was as if a dark shroud came down over our house—there were hushed conversations followed by loud fights. My father looked haggard and strained, my mother's drinking got worse. Binnie Milner accused my father of siphoning off funds from the corporation into his own three peat bog businesses, which he still maintained. There was a court case that lasted two years, during which time we lived with the threat of my father going to jail.

I was playing hopscotch on the front sidewalk when my father came home from giving testimony in court. "It must be so nice to be a child," he said. "You don't have a single care in the world, you don't have a single problem. I wish I were a child again."

Eventually, he was exonerated. Visiting him once in Vancouver, when I was studying in Toronto, he gave me the judge's summation to read. The judge declared my father to be credible and honest, judicious in his business dealings and generally above reproach.

As an adult, I realize two things about this story: first, it was a classic case of a multinational corporation taking over a small successful business (in this case my father's business expertise), getting all the benefits of the research and development, and then squashing the small business owner—a pattern that has existed on a wide scale since the Second World War. Second, Binnie Milner gave or sold shares in the corporation to all his cronies, the Vancouver business elites who would come out to shareholder meetings expressly to vote against my father. I'm pretty sure there was a large element of "get the Jew" in this.

7. And Back Up Again

He was planning to sue Binnie Milner all the way up to the Supreme Court of Canada when my mother had the stroke that left her with permanent brain damage. He sold his shares, was able to retire on the proceedings in his mid-forties and joined the Jewish golf and country club in West Vancouver. Soon, all his friends were Jewish, he played golf all the time, and my mother felt completely excluded. It was the beginning of the end of a marriage that had been anything but happy for so many years.

The lease on the golf course was expiring, and Jack took it upon himself to find land in Richmond and to design and build a new Jewish golf course. From there, he was only a short step away from building his own commercial course. He had the Midas touch and played the stock market to great financial gain—eventually he became a multimillionaire.

8. Atheism

I both knew and did not know that I was half Jewish. It was what psychologists call the "unthought known." Both my parents were atheists; both thought the nicest thing you could say about religion was that it is superstition. We celebrated Christmas and Easter as secular holidays, and as a child I went with my friends on Cypress Street to St. Faith's Anglican Church Sunday School. If I ever queried either parent, they both told me, in the most forthright way, that there was no such thing as God, still less an afterlife.

"See that log?" my father said, pointing to the fireplace. "When it's burnt, all that's left is the ashes, and that's exactly what's left when you die."

9. Six Million

We were the first family on Cypress Street to have a TV, and we all watched a lot in those early days. *Playhouse 90*, a weekly drama series that lasted an hour and a half, was a family favourite. Once, when I was thirteen or fourteen, I was watching it with my mother. The program showed documentary footage of Holocaust survivors, the now familiar images of emaciated prisoners and piles of dead bodies. There were dramatic re-enactments of Nazi concentration camps. I went into a kind of psychic shock. I ran out of the living room into the bathroom, locked the door, and sat sobbing on the edge of the bathtub. My father came home and heard me crying and persuaded me to open the door.

"You know, I'm Jewish," he said, "and you are half Jewish. If you'd lived in Germany twenty years ago, you would have been sent to a concentration camp." This information was relayed as matter-of-factly as if he'd been reading the evening news. There was no context given to the revelation, and no comfort.

I went through a brief period of trying to connect with my Jewish roots and joined B'nai B'rith Girls. One of the older girls, appalled at my ignorance, took over my Jewish education. I learned "Hatikvah," the national anthem of Israel, but every time we got to the line "Shnot alpayim" I was overcome with fits of giggles at the sound of the word *shnot*. My mentor was not thrilled with her protégé. I was not to become a born-again Jew.

10. Giving

In his sixties, my father told me that he had a plan to get the Order of Canada for himself. He would do this by giving money away. First, he would get the Key to the City of Vancouver, then some kind of province of British Columbia honour, and then the Order of Canada. He thought it would take him ten years. The plan was carried out to the letter.

For many years he was, at least locally, famous for his philanthropy. He bought naming rights to a wing of the Vancouver General Hospital and to the building housing the School of Social Work at the University of British Columbia. He bought a fleet of vans with his name on each of them for the Jack Bell Foundation, which was a non-profit that fostered carpooling before hardly anyone else was thinking about ways to solve urban traffic congestion. He gave seed money to build a longhouse for Indigenous students at UBC; again, long before it was in any way fashionable or even countenanced to fund resources for Indigenous Canadians.

His very first act of philanthropy was to approach Vancouver City Council and tell them he would match their funding if they built a shelter for women who were victims of domestic abuse or sexual assault, in the Downtown East Side of Vancouver. He always claimed that I was his conscience, that he saw me in his mind's eye when he made this proposal.

11. Kissy Kissy

"Give me a little kiss right here," he'd say, pointing to his cheek. Then he'd turn his head quickly and kiss whoever—me, his secretary, my sister's high school girlfriends—on the mouth.

At his own commercial golf course, where he took me for a tour every time I visited Vancouver, there was always a little ritual. He hugged the manager and got her to kiss him.

When I was sixteen, he told me he'd been in love with his secretary, Carol, for many years. I remember her wedding. He walked her down the aisle and gave her away to her new husband. I also remember her babysitting me when my father and mother went out. The patriarchy at work. I loved her—she was so much sweeter and more docile than my harsh, mean-spirited mother.

There were darker stories, rumours that he'd had his wallet stolen in New York, something involving a transgender sex worker. My best friend in high school came out a few years after we graduated. She was a gifted athlete and started playing golf at the Richmond Club, where she claimed my father offered to pay her to have sex with one of his woman friends so he could watch.

My nephew, his grandson, at age eleven was doing a school project on a family tree and asked my father about his past. My father pointed to a row of photograph albums and told him to look through them. One of them contained pornography—pictures he'd paid his housekeeper and her girlfriend to pose nude for.

12. That Dress

One day, my father and I were talking about American politics, and out of nowhere he said, "That little Jewish bitch brought down a great man!" It took me a moment to realize what he was talking about.

"Well," I said, "don't you think Clinton had something to do with it? Was at least half responsible, if not more?"

"Penis erectus non habet conscientiam," he said.

"What was that?"

"A stiff prick has no conscience."

13. Beowulf

I once took a course in Anglo-Saxon poetry. I fell in love with the earthiness, the grittiness, of this foundational language—the loneliness of its protagonists, their courage. It was, and remains for me, the truest expression of all that is good about masculinity.

"Remember when you took that course in Anglo-Saxon poetry," he said many times over the years. "What a waste of time that was! What possible use could there be in spending time reading a dead language that no one reads now?"

14. Divvy It Up

Still, there was a period of time, after the Binnie Milner debacle and before he began his campaign to buy himself the Order of Canada, when we were quite close. When I was an undergraduate at Dalhousie University in Halifax, he visited every few months and always took me and my friends out for lavish dinners. Cheques appeared in the mail, randomly, what he referred to as "divvies"—dividends. He gave me shares in some of his companies—his golf course and his cranberry and blueberry farms—and from time to time, presumably at his behest, these companies would declare a dividend, and I would get a cheque in the mail for a thousand dollars, or two thousand dollars, or once, five thousand dollars.

My friends deeply envied me. It didn't occur to me at the time there really were no strings attached; nothing was expected of me in return.

Once, however, when I was in the graduate English department at the University of Toronto, I passed on a four thousand dollar "divvie" to the women's committee of striking miners in Sudbury. This did trigger an outraged response on my father's part, but I merely shrugged.

"It was a divvie," I said. "It's not as if you gave it to me as a gift."

15. Paternalism 1.0

He called once, after I finally graduated, had become a mother, and was trying to figure out how to be an artist. After launching into a fifteen-minute, non-stop discourse on how successfully his various companies were doing, he asked: "And how are things in your little life?"

Shaking with anger, I confronted him.

"Oh, I'm sorry," he said, with glib insincerity. "I didn't mean to hurt your feelings."

I could hear him edit out the word "little" before "feelings."

"And by the way, how's what's-his-name?" (His name was Brian, my partner and the father of our child, Jack's grandchild.)

16. The Grift

When he was sixty-two my father met a twenty-two-year-old woman (younger than me) named Loretta. She called him Big Bucks Belitsky. They loved to golf and travelled all over the world. He set her up as a manager of one of his cranberry operations and bought her a house on Vancouver Island. But when they visited my brother in Malaysia, she went to Singapore by herself for a few days. My brother told me Jack paced anxiously and obsessively the whole time she was gone, worrying about her safety, wondering why she hadn't called him.

When he was in his eighties, as we walked around the sea wall together in Stanley Park, he told me some alarming stories. "She took my credit card and charged an entire trip to Seattle for herself, her mother, and her aunt. And she's writing cheques to herself from the cranberry company. She takes out small mortgage loans at high interest on that house I bought her in Nanoose—five, ten, fifteen thousand dollars. Of course I pay them off. But I love her so much, I'm so worried she'll just become a bag lady after I'm gone."

The next time we spoke I asked him if she was still taking money.

"Oh, I never said that! Or if I did, I made it up. Loretta is the most wonderful woman I've ever known. I'd give her anything, I love her."

That "anything" eventually became everything he had.

Every once in a while, a story would surface. A housecleaner found cheques on his desk that she had forged; my brother called the police, but they said unless my father laid a charge, there was nothing they could do. Another housekeeper told my sister that Loretta was being abusive, that she had seen her strike him. My sister called the elder abuse hotline, but again, they said he would have to lodge the complaint. We never knew what she'd done with the money because she always claimed to be broke. "If she at least stashed it in a Swiss bank account," my sister said. But none of us thought she was smart enough for that.

A pattern emerged. It seemed when she asked him for money and he refused, she threatened to leave, and he would capitulate. She was manipulating him more and more into cutting off contact with us, his three children.

17. Nothing to Lose but Your Chains

On one of his visits to Toronto over drinks on the roof of the Park Plaza Hotel, before a typically extravagant meal, I told him, with a mixture of trepidation and boldness, that I had become a member of the Communist Party of Canada.

"Oh," he said. "How proud your grandmother would be! You know, my mother, your *bubbeh*, used to run a Yiddish Socialist school in Montreal for all the Jewish children in the neighbourhood."

At a family reunion at my cousin's in Quebec, we were all sitting around telling stories about him.

"What a killing we made," my oldest cousin said. "When he gave us those shares who knew they'd triple in value."

"Oh Jack," my cousin Helen said in a reverent tone. "Uncle Jack was a Communist!"

He always maintained that the best form of government is a benevolent dictatorship, because poor people would have rights and benefits, but there would be none of the inefficiencies of liberal democratic governments. He hated the Soviet Union because it wasn't efficient, not because of its human rights violations. On the other hand, he thought Fidel Castro was the exemplar of a benevolent dictator.

18. Not Kosher

My father loved to eat and struggled with his weight, which he would address biannually with trips to a luxurious resort he called "the fat farm." His all-time favourite thing to eat was lobster. He loved taking me for a lobster dinner and telling me stories about previous epic lobster feeds.

"Before you were born your mother and I bought four lobsters from a fisherman and ate them in our motel room in Prince Edward Island. But in the middle of the night the shells started to smell, and I had to get up and take them out to the highway to the garbage. But oh my, it was worth it!" He became so engrossed in his stories he summoned the waiter. "Bring me another lobster!"

He had a generous spirit, with money and with time. He drove me places, met me at airports, helped me buy a car.

19. Straight Outta Jeanne-Mance (Two)

Waiting in line at a restaurant in Vancouver with my family, some people behind us were shown a table before we were. Jack had a tense, worried, angry look about him. I had a sudden, momentary glimpse of him at eighteen, straight out of the ghetto, ashamed, vulnerable, poor. I wonder if he always felt like an outsider, no matter how much money he made.

Yet this is the same man who, also at eighteen, charmed his way past the secretary of the President of Bell Canada and sold this powerful man a magazine subscription. Who talked down a gunman who charged into his office, persuading him to put the gun down and leave.

20. Memories are Made of This?

In 1989, when I was living in Big Sur, I began to experience flashbacks of sexual abuse by my father. They came more and more frequently, and the pain of these memories was more and more excruciating. Emotional and physical pain, pain that doubled me over; me begging for it to stop. It seemed that I wasn't alone—there were many other women at Esalen who were also remembering incest, and I started a support group. We all read Laura Davis' *The Courage to Heal*, a popular self-help book. I broke up, for the final time, with the man I'd had a tumultuous relationship with for four years, packed up me and my daughter, and headed for home.

Back in Toronto I found a therapist who believed my memories. (No one in the family believed me.)

I joined another support group. Eventually I cut my ties to my father and told him I wanted to sell my shares in his various companies. He took the sale of the shares as a deeply personal betrayal, far worse than the fact that I stopped speaking to him for seven years.

I don't know what to think about all this now, given the debunking of so called "false memories", and the criticism of therapists who believed their clients. (Sigmund Freud initially believed his clients, and then did a sharp *volte face* and said their stories of sexual assault were the fantasies of women wanting to have sex with their fathers.)

Were my memories, which were so alive, and viscerally true at the time, some transmission of the zeitgeist? A revenge fantasy? A way of separating from a certainly emotionally incestuous relationship with my father? All I know for certain is that the pain of those memories was excruciatingly real, and that the therapist who treated me helped me, for the first time, to become stable, to lead a more or less healthy adult life. And in that Toronto support group I met Terry, and together we helped each other heal from our respective familial wounds. When he was diagnosed ten years later with an incurable brain tumour, we got married.

Was my father a pedophile? I know he had no sexual boundaries when it came to being seductive with women and young girls. I know his deep patronization of me, his general lack of respect for women, was a source of inchoate fury for me for years, his charms be damned.

One day after the seven-year estrangement, my brother came to visit me in Toronto and, over dinner, begged me to resume contact with him. "He's old now," John said. "He can't hurt you anymore. It's breaking his heart, and it's breaking mine." He was weeping as he said these words. "Please, just get on a plane and go see him."

When I knocked on the door of his penthouse on the twenty-seventh floor, which overlooked English Bay and Stanley Park, he held out his arms for a hug. "Daddy's little girl," he said. I ducked away. "Come in," he said. "What would you like to drink?" "A glass of wine please." "How was your trip?" "Very pleasant," I replied. And so it went.

21. Denouement

In his early nineties, he wrote us a letter saying he and Loretta were moving and that he didn't want to have anything to do with us for a year. It was written in the style of a reality television star; we suspected she wrote it and got him to sign it. Although there was supposedly no contact, this man, who gave away millions, had to call my brother and ask us to pay his rent. Finally, the "old man's friend," pneumonia, came to pay a call, and as he lay dying in his hospital bed, I did a three-day vigil and whispered to him that I forgave him. But did I? Have I?

22. Legacy

A man who came from deep poverty, acquired a vast fortune, and let it be taken from him. Who left the world as he came into it, in penury. Who, having been generous to every panhandler who ever approached him on the street, became, at the end of his life, a beggar himself, continually asking friends and acquaintances for loans. A man who viewed all women as sexual prey, and was destroyed by a manipulating, predatory woman.

A man who had a daughter who loved and despised him in equal measure.

There but for fortune, go I.

And sometimes, going to sleep, I clutch a soft stuffed dog to my complicated heart.

MERCY AND ME

Green and sunlight and flashes of white as she runs. Simple joy, simple energy, tearing back and forth, zooming to me to thank me for letting her run off the leash, dashing ahead to show me how far from me she's not afraid to go. It's a dirt road, probably once a logging road, with few of the mosquitoes that have plagued us all summer; this is third or fourth growth forest. I don't know who owns the land. Blue sky into infinity. Everything sparkles. I walk without pain. The dog and I are one spirit, one entity. My canine soulmate. It's cooler today, the air a little crisp. The dog loves the coolness, a white blur as she careens back and forth, her fur blowing a little in the wind her running makes. I can walk faster in this weather; I can walk forever; after so many years I can walk without pain, in my knee, in my feet, ankles, calves, thighs, shoulders, neck. Absence of pain is presence of delight, of freedom, just me and the dog, the sky and the road and the trees. Even God is smiling at the sight of we two creatures, Mercy and me, on a summer morning, in the woods.

"EVERYTHING SOLID MELTS INTO AIR": SO-CALLED MENTAL, SO-CALLED ILLNESS

The First Time

At twenty-three, I found myself living in Oxford, England. I have no recollection of going there, or of how I found my three house-mates. Tony, with whom I was sleeping, was a very bad painter from Australia. Roy was a very bad writer, and his wife Barbara had a job in publishing that kept the household more or less going. My predecessor in Tony's bed had committed suicide. Although I never knew her, her shadow tinged our lives.

I graduated from Dalhousie University the year before and panicked at the thought of going back to Berwick in the Annapolis Valley with my then husband, Henry. He was running a peat bog operation for my father, and there was nothing for me to do. Also, I was having an affair. I fled first to Montreal for Expo summer, with my lover Michel, and then to Europe where I met up with and began an affair with Michel's best friend Peter. Michel and Peter had both been accepted into Stanford to do graduate work, but I, being married to Henry, hadn't thought of applying anywhere. I just vaguely assumed that after my BA I would settle down and have a baby in the Annapolis Valley. It's astonishing to me now, how little I thought of the future.

So Henry was back in Berwick, having a relationship with a sixteen-year-old girl, and Peter and Michel had gone off to school. I bummed around Europe on my own for several months, staying in youth hostels, becoming increasingly lonely and unmoored. I didn't know where my home was, where I could return to. Certainly not to either of my separated parents in Vancouver. Going back to school—somewhere, anywhere—seemed the only option. I decided I would take the Oxford entrance examinations, since I was living there anyway, and it would be quite a feather in my cap to get into Oxford and lord it over Michel and Peter at lowly Stanford.

I recall being in the study of a woman who was in charge of admissions, a genuine Oxford don. The room was shabbily elegant in that English way, full of books, floral fabrics, and tea. The phone rang. She excused herself and answered the call. "Oh hello, David," she said, "how lovely to hear from you." I wanted all this—the study, the cashmere twin set, the tweed skirt, and her friendship with David, which I construed as non-sexual, this warm, beloved friendship of which nothing was required but acknowledgement of shared history and interests. I imagined they read the same books, saw the same movies. She recommended that I get a tutor to prepare for the exams and gave me the phone number of a retired professor, another woman don.

This woman, however, told a different story. Her study was as dishevelled as she was, crumbs and unwashed dishes everywhere. She emitted a strange odor, and always seemed to have some leftover greens stuck in her front teeth. Still, I had few other choices. I continued to study her reading list, met with her weekly, and fell deeper and deeper into a numb depression. Reality felt like a wet shroud of heavy black fabric, pressing down on me. I went for long aimless walks in the constant drizzle of an English summer, which felt like November.

Of course, I failed the exams. I wasn't surprised. It confirmed my certainty that I myself was the failure—a failure as a woman, as a thinker, as someone with agency of any kind. My family, my husband and my various lovers had all betrayed me, that is to say, they none of them had rescued me. I was twenty-three, and my life was over. I felt old. There was no point in anything, still less in living.

I swallowed a hundred aspirin and went for a long walk in the rain, along a meadow that in memory was as dead as I felt. I returned to the house and told Tony what I had done. I remember the ghastly look on his face at the thought of a second lover killing herself. He called Barbara and she came home from work and took me to the hospital, and I was referred to a mental institution. This place specialized in something called "sleep therapy," which involved drugging patients so heavily that they slept for weeks on end, woken up only to eat their meals. Given the quality of the food, perhaps they preferred to sleep. Fortunately this wasn't the recommended therapy for me, and when my father learned I was there, he flew to England, scooped me up and took me to Toronto, where he had come to know that I could get into the graduate English department if I successfully completed a makeup year.

I later found out, in another mental hospital, that aspirin will very rarely kill you. A very young woman I met there was an expert on suicide methods that don't work. To this end, she once swallowed a thousand aspirin, and of course, lived to tell the tale, not without pride.

The Second Time

It was the late sixties. I did that makeup year and started my graduate classes. There seemed to be a very big disjuncture between the genteel, *belle-lettrist* old gentleman's club that was the graduate English department at the University of Toronto, and the riotous, momentous events swirling around us—anti-war demonstrations, hippie love-ins, and most significantly, feminism. I was studying iconography in Spencer's book-length poem, *The Faerie Queene*, which I eventually planned to write my doctoral dissertation on, and moonlighting reading Marx, Engels, Lenin, Mao, Frantz Fanon—and Gloria Steinem, Robin Morgan, Kate Millett, Germaine Greer. I was chairman (not yet chairperson) of the Graduate English Students Association. I was often summoned to the departmental chairman's office, to be given sherry and a lengthy, circuitous, momentous discussion about, for example, whether he should authorize a payment of $20 for more postage to send out announcements of student events.

On weekends I dropped acid with my draft dodger boyfriend, who was a big leftist man on campus. I traded in my tweed skirts and sweater sets for workboots and plaid flannel shirts, grew my hair long and wore it in braids. On alternate days, I wore micro mini-skirts and ropes and ropes of beaded necklaces, my long hair streaming down my back.

Reading the *Communist Manifesto* for the first time, with its thrilling first sentence—"There is a spectre haunting Europe, and that spectre is Communism"—I felt the gears of my mind shifting. Everything that had confused and frightened me about a world that seemed irrational and meaningless now took on great clarity. Karl Marx was the man with the plan, and I became his willing acolyte. It is possible to understand how society works, why there is such inequality—indeed it is a science, scientific socialism! I started going to protest meetings, speaking up for the first time, trembling with nervousness and excitement. But my Marxist boyfriend from Brooklyn, with his black curly hair and revolution-ready moustache, didn't seem too happy with my newfound voice. Reading Eldridge Cleaver, I learned that the only place for a woman in the revolution is on her back.

I got behind in my coursework and asked my modern novel professor if I could write my major paper over the summer. I wanted to try and figure out why I detested Virginia Woolf. In a rage against everything I considered to be bourgeois, I had thrown all my poetry books and novels down the basement stairs. I read the Woolf canon, and unsurprisingly, *A Room of One's Own* had the same effect on me as the *Communist Manifesto*. I fell in love, in spite of myself, with her novels, and wrote my paper parsing and extolling her prose. By the end of the summer, I was a feminist. A Marxist feminist. Sheepishly, I retrieved my poetry books and novels from where they lay in a heap on the basement floor and put them back on my book-shelf. I both loved and despised the canon of English literature. I took speed and stayed up all night reading *Vanity Fair*, Shakespeare, Milton—and started writing political pamphlets.

I moved in with the draft dodger boyfriend, took more acid and smoked more pot. I didn't sleep or eat much. Things got more intense, more speeded up. I was sleeping around a lot; it was the free love era. I'm not sure how it happened, but I had a one-night stand with a guy called Don Cumming. He was staying with friends of his in a gorgeous old mansion on Madison Avenue in Toronto's Annex neighbourhood. I think what tipped me over was a weird obsession with him. I started to believe that, if I travelled the subway all the way to the east, I would see the *dawn coming,* and would be united in a sacred marriage with Don Cumming. Then I became convinced that if I stayed on the subway long enough I would encircle the globe. I was talking to all kinds of random strangers, telling them that God and Dog were the same thing, that spelling forwards and backwards was the linguistic equivalent of circumnavigating the globe on the subway.

A stranger, an older man, invited me back to his apartment in Scarborough, and I went willingly. He was, I think, a superintendent of some kind, because he had two phones in his place, which he continually referred to as his "inside line" and his "outside line." I told him I too had an inside and an outside line. At dawn, he kicked me out. I remember walking in the early morning rain, belting out Gordon Lightfoot's song. At some point I got into a taxi, and voices were speaking to me from the dispatcher. "She came in on a six," a man's voice said sagely, and I knew this to be the absolute truth, that six was my portal number, the conduit between this world and the next. I found my way back to the house on Madison, pleading to see Don Cumming. He turned up—perhaps someone called him, and I remember the look of revulsion on his face. From then on, visions flooded my psyche. Images of the harmony of the black and the white race, of Lenin and Rosa Luxemburg, of Milton Acorn and Gwendolyn MacEwen.

There were various people around. When I saw friends I recognized, their faces seemed washed clean of all pain. There was only their inner transcendent beauty, which dazzled and thrilled me. But one looked like a trickster; I believed that my boyfriend, the draft dodger from Brooklyn, was Satan personified, and convinced everyone not to let him near me. One friend wanted me to take a bath. I agreed, but only if she got in with me, and only if she obeyed my command to "keep your shirt on," which seemed a momentous requirement for all of life: just keep your shirt on. My next to last conscious memory of this stage of things was of us facing each other in the tub, our wet shirts stuck to our bodies.

Then suddenly I was in the street, in a straitjacket, being hustled into the back of an ambulance by two police officers. I hauled off and kicked one of them in the butt—I guess this is the only time I can get away with that, I said, laughing. (I learned later that the next day, one of my friends was at a demonstration and saw this same cop—"Hey, how's your friend?" he asked.)

I came to in a hospital ward with two other young women, each playing a radio at full volume on different stations. I had been heavily drugged and felt a keen nostalgia for the great insights and visions I had so recently had, but which were now lost to me.

I gradually learned that my friends had coalesced into two groups who were at bitter odds as to what should be done. One group, including the woman who kept her shirt on, and the friends of Don Cumming, had read R.D. Laing, who believed that insanity was actually a sane response to an insane world. They thought I should stay there, and they would gain wisdom from my oracular remarks. Crazy was groovy. The other group of friends I'd known longer and were closer to me. They were gravely concerned that I hadn't eaten or slept for a week. The University of Toronto staff psychiatrist was summoned. My father was there at this point, begging this doctor to tell him what to do. The psychiatrist, however, was in the groovy crazy camp. My father called my sister, a psychotherapist, who told him to get me to a hospital immediately if he wanted to save my life. She came from Berkeley to see me in the hospital, and allayed my terror that I would be given shock treatment. You have the opposite problem, she said. You're not depressed, you're psychotic. And indeed, I was diagnosed with having a full-scale psychotic break, and was put first on Thorazine, and then on Lithium.

I spent two months on that psych ward, earning walking privileges by finally capitulating and agreeing to wear a bra. I spent my twenty-seventh birthday there. The chair of the English Department came and visited me. We sat opposite one another in two wheelchairs that had been left at the end of the hall. It felt like the gulag of mental health care. I was grateful to my friends and family for getting me there, though, frightened by the thought that if things had gone on, I might have died. I had been taking the antibiotic tetracycline for a skin condition, and I found out that it destroys the bacteria in your stomach that metabolize vitamin B. There was a school of thought, much touted by my Marxist friends, that believed mental illness, especially psychosis, was caused by a vitamin B deficiency. I swallowed vast handfuls of Vitamin B for about a year, which turned my skin a dayglo orange. I was by then firmly in the pro-hospital, materialist view of mental illness camp.

I returned to school but knew that the graduate English department at the University of Toronto would never let me into their almost all male club, now more than ever. I transferred to York University, joined the Communist Party of Canada, and set up my Marxist book table every Wednesday in Ross Hall. I don't think I ever sold a single pamphlet, let alone a book. They were all from Progress Publishers in Moscow, the most dreary designs and cheapest paper ever to grace the world of publishing. But I got to talk to lots of people with whom I engaged in bitter arguments. My friend Mary, also in the English Department, came and sat with me each week. She was—and is—a devout High Anglican, but I felt a kinship with her because she was the only other person in the department who felt a part of something larger than herself. I called our conversations, which mostly consisted of gossiping about students and faculty, the Commie-Christian Dialogue.

For years, I was afraid that I would have another psychotic break, and whenever I felt anxious I'd take Valium. But something underneath always tugged at me, something that made me yearn for the intensity and truth of the visions I'd had, something I never confessed to anyone.

I was writing my doctoral dissertation on political theatre and was in a relationship with a Grade Seven dropout and an alcoholic Party member from Thunder Bay. It wasn't the most dysfunctional relationship I've ever had, but close. He was incredibly funny; we spent every weekend getting drunk and stoned, listening to the Rolling Stones, and, in his case, sleeping around. I constantly broke up with him, did my own sleeping around for revenge, and then we'd get back together. Other equally difficult relationships followed. At some point, it occurred to me that I could use some help, and although it took me a few years, and becoming a mother, I finally started seeing a therapist.

To this kind and sage woman, I allowed both my fear of having another breakdown, and my longing for the part of myself that got left behind. She told me there was a man in Big Sur, California, at the Esalen Insitute, who believed that psychosis was a spontaneous initiation into shamanism. He was giving workshops, and Big Sur was a gorgeous place to visit.

The Third Time

Stanislav Grof was Europe's counterpart to Timothy Leary. He had been doing research on LSD in Czechoslovakia until the government cut his funding and shut him down, much as Harvard shut down Timothy Leary and Richard Alpert, later known as Baba Ram Dass. Esalen was the epicenter of everything New Age—Rolfing realignment therapy, Tarot cards, meditation, yoga, spiritual healing by touch, nude massages, rebirthing—where you simulated coming down the birth canal and reviving "memories" of your birth. Not surprisingly, I took to all this just as I had with Marx and Virginia Woolf—I dove in with my whole being. Eventually, when my daughter was five, I spent two months there. I worked in the organic garden, work being a euphemism as we paid Esalen for the privilege. I did medicine wheels and sweat lodges and solitary vision quests in the Ventana mountains. (This was before anyone white there thought about cultural appropriation.) At the end of one of our month-long group sessions, we did a final hike, and I told a friend, I don't really feel anything, I just feel normal and ordinary. For you that's an altered state, he said.

There was so much swirling around in my psyche I scarcely noticed I was actually hallucinating, in much the same way I had during the psychotic episode I'd had fifteen years before. I saw seeds sprouting out of ashtrays and was convinced that one of the group leaders working in the garden was transmitting messages to me from "the other side." When I told someone about the flowers sprouting up everywhere, real and imagined, she said, you're lucky, most of us are taking drugs to have experiences like that. When I confessed to the group leader that I thought he was a vessel for messages to me from the universe, he said he was honoured and flattered.

I think, if these things were happening in Toronto, I would have ended up in a psychiatric ward again. With me through all of this was my then five-year-old daughter, who basically had the run of Esalen as I was hardly competent to take care of her. I like to think, though, that it was nonetheless a better experience for her not to be separated from me, as she would have been if I had been hospitalized again. I came to refer to this so-called breakdown as a breakthrough. For all its own craziness, I'm grateful for Esalen and its steady stream of New Age leaders and followers, for creating a container for me as I went through these strange, but oddly liberating, experiences.

Also, a seemingly innocuous activity I started at Esalen began a parallel journey of momentous importance in my life and my future "sanity." I found a rubber stamp in the office where I was working, a stamp with one word on it: VOID. We had been exploring the idea of the void in some of my workshops—was the void, as the ground zero of consciousness, empty or full, frightening, or benign? I began playing with the word, making designs with it, collaging images onto the designs. I made a series called A(void) Art. I started to collect dozens of rubber stamps, including one of a salamander, which in various cultures rises up unscathed from fire.

One day I drove into Monterey and went to an art supply store, where I discovered two magical substances. The first was a "resist," a kind of paste you can brush on and paint over, and it resists the paint. So you could make different-coloured texts. Even more transformational was acrylic matte medium, which you could use to collage paper and fabric onto wood. Playing with these materials and creating works with them gave me a childlike joy that I hadn't ever experienced as an adult.

I think they saved me. I had happened on a mysterious gate, an opening to my unconscious that didn't frighten me, didn't disconnect me from reality. On the contrary, making these pieces connected me to a deep sense of reality, and of myself.

The Fourth Time

I remained in Big Sur off and on for four years, living in The Stone House on Gorda Mountain, a house built by William Randolph Hearst and left to his hairdresser. Subsequently it was owned by a succession of hippies and mountain men. Big Sur is where old hippies go to stay stoned, growing the strongest sensimilla in the world. I tried it a few times, but it just re-started the hallucinations. I was in the most supremely dysfunctional of all my dysfunctional relationships with men, this time with an alcoholic, emotionally abusive stoner who made a living, such as it was, foraging chanterelle mushrooms in the mountains, fishing illegally for abalone, and dealing drugs.

I got a Canada Council grant that enabled me to live in Big Sur for a year, and then worked at the little one-room schoolhouse, where my daughter was a pupil, delivering a cultural enrichment program for Grades One to Twelve. I continued to take workshops at Esalen, hang out in the nude baths, get nude massages, and, when I wasn't writing a play, repeatedly break up with my boyfriend until he promised to get clean and sober. Then we'd get back together until the next time. It wasn't all bad. On weekends I'd take my daughter and her friends to the beaches only locals knew about, and we'd all play in the waves for hours. We hiked the mountain trails, and I made some lasting friendships. But I was becoming very troubled by the fact that all the adults were stoned all the time and didn't seem to notice or care that teenaged boys, some as old as twenty, were having sex with girls as young as eleven. I started an Alateen program at the school, since almost all the children's parents were always drunk and/or stoned. A boy told me he was offered cocaine at a birthday party when he was five. I was worried about my daughter, who was now nine years old.

Then, seemingly out of nowhere, I started having vivid flash-backs of sexual abuse, by both my mother and my father. These memories, if that's what they were, were so unbearably realistic and painful, I would be physically beaten down for days. They started coming faster and became more horrific. I believed them to be fac-tually true, and started a group at Esalen for incest survivors. I broke up with the stoned, drunk mountain man for the last time, scooped up my daughter, and headed back to Toronto. I got her settled in school, spent the summer repairing my house, which the tenants had wrecked, and continued to have hallucinatory memories.

I joined a Twelve-Step program for incest survivors, where I met and eventually married Terry, another survivor with stories even more bizarre than mine. We spent ten happy, and for the first time for me, stable years before he died of a brain tumour. I have since come to doubt those memories, yet I can't doubt how real they felt, nor the level of physical and mental anguish they brought with them. Had I not had those memories, and had I not believed them, I wouldn't have met that most wonderful man, or had those happy years with him.

There has been a great deal of controversy surrounding "re-covered memories" of childhood sexual abuse, so called "False Memory Syndrome," and they, and therapists who encouraged them, have been debunked. But like the visions I had in my so-called psychotic break in my twenties, there was a truth there beyond the ordinary, which to this day mystifies me. Were the memories a sign of mental illness? Was I delusional? I wish my husband had lived long enough for me to have this conversation with him.

These were also artistically productive years. I founded Art Starts, a neighbourhood community art centre, still thriving more than thirty years later, and took life drawing classes at the Toronto School of Art. I have no talent as an artist—it was a struggle to learn to draw, but a joyous one. My technical skills, such as they are, were hard won, but I've never lacked for creativity. We had to take a course on anatomy for artists, learn to identify and draw the bones and muscles, and hand in a drawing of a skeleton. I got my partner to take a full-length photograph of me in profile, superimposed a skeleton on to my body, blew the image up in sections, printed and glued them together to make a life size self portrait with a skeleton on it. The exercise became a poignant memento mori.

In the succeeding years, I made and exhibited paintings, draw-ings, installations, videos, web-based projects, and large-scale com-munity art projects, sometimes involving hundreds of people. I never again feared I would disconnect from ordinary reality. As a friend said once, I can swim in and out of my unconscious like a dolphin.

The Fifth—and So Far, the Last Time

The first six or seven years after my husband died were years of the unmitigated agony of grief, and also years of a spiritual awakening of much greater profundity than anything I experienced in my Big Sur years. Me, the work-boot sporting, plaid-shirt wearing, Marxist Feminist—and the nude bathing Gestalt therapy spouting New Ager—wound up a devout member of the Anglican Church. As my faith deepened, I searched for ways I could be of service. I volun-teered for a few years at Bereaved Families of Ontario as a peer sup-port grief counselor, and then one day heard the phrase "spiritual direction." Just as years before I somehow "found" myself in Oxford, and then in Big Sur, I "found" myself at Regis College, the Jesuit College in the Toronto School of Theology, undertaking a diploma in Spiritual Direction, without really having any idea what it was about.

The kind women faculty, both lay and religious, and the Jesuit priests, taught Christianity based on social justice, love and the idea that God is present in all things in the created world. Since I felt I had no need to prove myself academically—to myself or to others—I began to hand in drawings and creative writing exercises instead of papers. With one or two exceptions, this was embraced and re-warded with high marks. I felt an immense sense of homecoming. My very soul flourished. Indeed, I was keenly aware much of the time that I did, in fact, have a soul, a soul I could take out for walks, a soul I could read poetry with, a soul I could pray with.

I had taken up the habit of drinking a single malt scotch at the end of every day, around five o'clock. It marked the transition from the day of work and study to the evening. I call it liturgical hooch, a ritual, a ritual being anything you repeat with intention. For the first six months I was at Regis College, every day when I drank my scotch, I would be overcome with a sense of the tender mystery at the heart of the world, and I would break down and cry. Sometimes I would cry deep sobs, sometimes gentle tears, but cry I did. After my husband died, I felt a similar sense of travelling to the heart of exist-ence, but there I found only darkness and profound meaninglessness. The universe was nothing but anarchy, randomness. But in those Regis months of weeping, existence itself trembled with the most pure and poignant beauty, a love so tender it could only be divine. I often had a sensation of being enfolded in great white wings.

I had no idea what was happening to me. I came across a book by Kay Redfield Jamison about artists and bipolar illness. She talked about a milder form of bipolar called cyclothymia and provided a handy checklist. I checked every box. So that's it, I thought—I'm a mildly bipolar artist. But about five months into this period of daily weeping I described what was happening to one of my professors, a religious sister I had befriended and whom I had invited over for dinner. I think you're having a mystical experience, she said. I didn't

have a clue what that meant. She recommended a book called
Mysticism and Resistance by a German theologian named Dorothee
Soelle. This author also had a checklist of the characteristics of a mystical experience. Again, I checked every box. I was struck by how
two exceptionally different narratives could describe the same experience. Did I want to think of myself as someone with a pathol-
ogy, or a mystic? Was I having a mental breakdown or a spiritual
awakening? Disability or epiphany? Breakdown or breakthrough?

Ever since I heard that voice coming through the taxi driver's
dispatch, I've felt a strange and profound affinity for the number six,
my portal number. Perhaps, having come in on a six, I will go out on
a six. Perhaps there is, after all, one more installment—the sixth time,
the transformation from this life into the next, the final removal of
the veil. I hope that my so-called mental so-called illnesses have
given me the wisdom to face that last breakthrough with all the
courage and equanimity I will need.

LIFTOFF

I had begged my mother to leave the hall light on, and leave the door a little bit open, claiming night terrors. Earlier I had secreted my book under my pillow. As soon as I heard her footsteps going down the stairs, I pulled the book out, flopped down on the bed with my head pointing toward the foot, and put it in the thin band of light coming in the door from the hall light. This was a nightly ritual. As soon as I heard someone coming up the stairs, I put the book back under the pillow, got under the covers, and pretended to be asleep. My brother and sister were seven and nine years older than me, and of course were allowed to stay up much later. To this day I sometimes have the suspicion there is a party going on somewhere and I wasn't invited.

With my book, though, I could fall into another reality, lose myself—and my martyred sense that my family was perpetrating a grievous injustice by making me go to bed when everyone else was still up. It was the perfect liftoff. Anyone walking down the street could see that there was a light on in the upstairs hallway, but they would never suspect that I was time-travelling, shape-shifting and reincarnating in multitudes of universes. I read and re-read all the children's classics, *The Secret Garden*, the Anne books, *The Princess and the Goblin*. We were allowed to take five books a week from the library, and it was always a challenge not to read them all in the first few days, so I tried to save them for my nighttime ritual. My older sister had a bookcase full of what we now call YA, which I regularly raided. And if I did run out of library books I could always cull from my brother's vast collection of Better Little Books as a last resort.

Though I didn't know it at the time, fiction was building an important spiritual muscle: empathy.

Reading, especially clandestine reading, was my very own private spaceship.

EARLY BIRD

1. The Clock

For my eighth birthday I was given an alarm clock. My mother read into the depths of night and slept until noon; I suspect she wanted me to have a way of waking up on time for school. This clock had a little bird on it, a robin (presumably also why my parents gave it to me), which endlessly tugged at a worm in time to the ticking of the clock. I was fascinated by this and watched it bobbing up and down each night before I fell asleep. The clock had a name printed on it: "Early Bird," as in "The early bird catches the worm." But this robin never did catch the worm; perhaps that's why I too am a night owl and late riser.

I searched for years for this clock. I told my partner Frank about it because he goes to used car swap meets and prowls the flea markets there. He's able to find anything, eventually—except the Early Bird clock. He hunted for it for years. He did find someone who had one, but they weren't willing to sell it. Otherwise, as far as we knew, the clock no longer existed.

Then, a few years ago, I drove to Owen Sound to photograph my old friend David Sereda for my art project, *Missing You*. I photographed David in his early fall garden, a profusion of gorgeous flowers and vegetables. He and his husband Stuart live in an old farmhouse full of interesting antiques. I was shown to the guest room, and what did I see on the windowsill? The Early Bird clock. Exactly as I re- membered it, except the bird was motionless. I immediately texted Frank, who urged me to offer to buy it. But it turned out that it was the only memento David had saved from his grandmother. We struck a deal—I would borrow it and see if it could be repaired so the little robin could move again, and then return it.

It took Frank over a year to find a clock repair shop that could make a new spring for it. (The original spring was not to be found.) He wanted to give it to me for Christmas, but I had to be satisfied with a paper rendition, a photo of the clock with a little cut out robin I could manually move up and down. Finally, the clock repair shop owner called him, and he gave it to me on Valentine's Day. At last, I can watch the little robin eternally trying to pull up the worm. I still find it fascinating to watch, for reasons I can't explain.

Of course, Frank wanted me to give him David's contact informa- tion so he could write to him and offer to buy it. And of course I re- fused. The next time I see David I will return it, regretful but happy that it now works and he can enjoy his grandmother's memento.

This story has all the elements of Frank's personality, and of our relationship. Frank can fix anything. He rescues microwave ovens from the garbage and repairs them and gives them to Goodwill. My house and my cottage run like well-oiled machines because Frank sees problems before they happen. All the small, annoying things that are the bane of a single woman's existence—a light bulb I can't reach; an oven that won't turn on; a deck that needs boards replaced; a leaky faucet—because you can never find anyone to fix them, are no longer the irritating little headaches they used to be.

2. The Man

I met him in January 2011, eight years after the death of my husband Terry and four years after the death of his wife Edna. That Christmas had in some ways been the hardest of the excruciating Christmases since Terry's death. I spent it with my sister and her family and, as much as they tried to make me feel loved and welcome, all I could feel was my own loneliness and seemingly unending grief.

I wasn't idle in those eight years. I'd done several art projects and one-woman shows. It was one of the most creative times of my life. And I'd done some online dating, mostly disastrous. Then, just after New Year, I got a message on the OKCupid site, and saw a picture of Frank, standing on a ladder, putting the last nail in the four-car garage he'd built. Wearing a tool belt. This is a good look on a man. He said in his note that he had first seen my profile on July 7 of the previous summer; he had dated three women since then, but there was something about me that just made him want to get to know me. He claims, although I don't remember this, that I sent a one-line answer: "What took you so long?"

On one of our early dates he was coming to my house and we planned to go out to dinner. I dressed carefully and even put on makeup, something I rarely do. Just as I went to answer the door, I realized I still had on my sheepskin slippers. No time to change! I opened the door. Frank did a quick once-over, and said, "I really like those slippers." His favourite adjective is "comfy."

After a few encounters, I asked if cohabitation was a deal breaker. He looked surprised because he just assumed that I would move in with him. He and Edna rebuilt and restored a house in Thornhill that the previous owner had gutted, and which they bought for a song. The floors come from old red pine boards that had originally been in the St. Lawrence Market in the fifties. The railings are from an old church. The house accomplishes the rare feat of being both spacious (it's enormous—3,400 square feet) and cozy. It's on three-quarters of an acre; the front yard is like a park, with old crabapple, magnolia and birch trees, and massive lilac bushes. Two blocks east of Yonge, and on the edge of a ravine, it's quiet and peaceful.

But it's in Thornhill, a forty-five minute car trip from my 1896 Victorian row house in the Annex. Just as his house is perfect for him, so mine is perfect for me. Only seventeen feet wide, it has a large second floor sitting room and bedroom, and a studio on the third floor. It's not just the house—my life, my work and all my friends are downtown. When Terry died, I had to rebuild my life from the ground up. I couldn't even walk in our old neighbourhood without being assailed by memories of our life together. Eventually I sold our house and moved into this house and into the start of a new life, a process that took three years. That was almost fifteen years ago, and I know that if I gave up my house and moved into Frank's, and if anything, God forbid, were to happen to him, I do not have it in me to start yet another life all over again. I need to preserve the one I created for myself from the ashes of my relationship with Terry.

3. The Relationship

Now I find, to my chagrin, that I'm merely part of a demographic— older couples in monogamous relationships, living apart. Frank comes downtown once a week, and I go to Thornhill every weekend. It's like having a little vacation in the country.

When we're apart, Frank is always improving his house, building a studio in the attic, a storage shed in the yard, a fibreglass roof over the patio so he can barbecue in the rain and snow. And I beaver away at my art projects and my writing in my home studio and am sustained by all the friendships I have nurtured over the years.

It's the daily and weekly rituals that make the scaffolding of our relationship. We always stop for a drink at five o'clock, me with my single malt scotch, he with his rum and coke. We talk over the day, and I rest my legs on his lap. Often, I just lie back and have a little half hour power nap. On Saturday nights I go skating at the Thornhill arena. Frank patiently watches me, and always praises me after.

On Sunday mornings Frank and my dog Mercy walk me to church, then come and meet me after for the coffee hour, and we walk home together. Mercy is much petted and adored by members of the congregation, who have dubbed her "The Anglican Dog."

We'd only been together a month or two when Joe and his wife Jen, two of Frank's oldest friends, came to visit from Newfoundland. Years later Frank told me Joe pulled him aside and told him in urgent tones that he should break up with me. Apparently we're both Type A personalities, and Joe told him it could never work. He had a point. We are both fiercely stubborn and enamoured of being in the right. We can fight over the most mundane, picayune subjects.

Frank had parked his car, at that point a boat-sized Lincoln Town Car, beside my little Suzuki Aerio in my back lane.

> Robin: Your car is too close to my neighbour's car. She
>   doesn't have enough space to get out easily.
> Frank: I'm inside your property line.
> Robin: No, you're too close.
> Frank: I can get a measuring tape and prove it to you. I'm
>   within the legal property line.
> Robin: It's not the letter of the law, it's the spirit of the law.
>   Staying on good terms with my neighbour is more
>   important than six inches of parking space, or
>   where the fuck the property line is.
> Frank: I'm telling you, I'm within my rights.
> Robin: Please JUST MOVE YOUR FUCKING CAR
>   SIX INCHES CLOSER TO MINE!!
> Frank: YOU'RE WRONG. MY CAR IS PERFECTLY
>   FINE WHERE IT IS!!

After several years of this, with me feeling ashamed and exhausted every time, we both seem to have reached the conclusion that being right isn't worth the wear and tear of the fights. One or both of us heads it off at the pass, leaves the room and waits until the rage abates about, for example, how to load the dishwasher correctly.

But there's another order of fights we haven't resolved yet. Like the battles over who's right, they are generic, and always involve what I perceive as Frank pushing my boundaries, and me reacting instinctively, and badly, before I realize what's happened. I had a mother who I remember from earliest childhood as wanting to control me. I hated her touching me, and worse, when I was a teenager, telling me what to do. Intimacy issues anyone? Frank likes to watch me cook and until I cured him of the habit (i.e. yelled at him often enough), would lift lids and change the burner temperature and generally supervise me. I am as klutzy in what I like to call "the world of things" as he is adept, but I still don't like to be watched and told what to do, or how to do it. This can be tricky because I often indeed don't know how to back up the car competently, or open jars, or store wineglasses so they won't break. But I want the freedom to ask for help, rather than have my klutziness watched over and anticipated. I end up yelling, Frank ends up sulking, and the evening is ruined. A work in progress.

Do all couples have these kinds of fights? Or are we just not very evolved?

Relationships are hard; I'm fond of quoting Garth in *Wayne's World 2*: "Relationships. Not for the timid." You're forced to learn things about yourself you wish you didn't have to, but even though the change is painful, it's for the better. Being with Frank has made me, albeit usually kicking and screaming, a better person. It takes a long time—years, I think—to get to know another person, to be able to sidestep their sharp angles and welcome their soft parts.

4. The End

A therapist once told me that in every relationship there's a pursuer and a pursued, and it's useful to know which one you are. I always thought that Terry was the pursuer, that he loved me more than I loved him, that my fears of intimacy forestalled my giving him my all. But when I found out he was going to die, all that evaporated in a second. I knew that my love for him was infinite and eternal, no matter how irritated I might be. The irritation was just ego. My higher self loved him unreservedly. Still, I learned that I need to be the one pursued.

When he's not driving me nuts, Frank is sweet and generous. If he leaves on a Thursday morning before I get up, I know that all the snow and ice will be brushed and scraped off my car. On winter evenings he always has a blazing fire in his wood-burning fireplace. In the summer he can be counted on to go on long walks with me and Mercy. When I cook, he cleans the kitchen impeccably. He doesn't like going to movies but will drive me to the Richmond Hill cinema and pick me up after.

As they say in Twelve Step programs, it works if you work it. Who would have thought that a downtown artist and a suburban scientist, who met on an internet dating site, would have an adventure together going on for ten years and counting? Frank just turned eighty, plays tennis twice a week, and is working with York University to bring one of his many patented inventions to market. He got a PhD in Aerospace Science but never strayed from his working-class Regina roots. His favourite food is scalloped potatoes served with macaroni and cheese, the Friday night treat of his childhood, when there wasn't much money for food by the end of the week. He was ten before they had indoor plumbing. I was a child of economic, if not emotional, privilege. Once, Frank came home with steaks he'd bought on sale at Food Basics. I fried them and fried them some more, but they just wouldn't brown, and they were impossible to cut. I figured out that they must have been injected with water to plump them up. If I bring meat I've bought at the farmer's market, it's always: "Oh yeah, meat from happy cows at three times the price!"

In spite of all these differences, we love each other to the moon and back. To the moon, Alice!

Love, like time, is a mystery. Unlike the world of my Early Bird clock, the real robin catches the worm. The worm dies, and the bird dies too. Age brings me closer to my own mortality. I alternate between being in denial, living as much as I can in the present, and contemplating the inevitable. Which of us will die first? Which is worse, to die, or be left behind to grieve? Both Frank and I know the inevitable, terrifying calamity that hides in the shadows, waiting to claim one of us. Knowing this, how is it even possible that we can argue, speak harsh words? What if the harsh word is the last? Perhaps the true, human miracle is that we can keep on loving one another, knowing as no one else does each other's frail, flawed, broken selves. Knowing that with each passing day, as that little bird bobs up and down, our deepening love only presages a deeper loss.

POST PANDEMIC POSTSCRIPT

Our ship, which we had managed to keep afloat for twelve years, finally broke apart on the shoals of money, control, and temperament. The enforced cohabitation during COVID was just too much pressure on our two combustible personalities. I always knew that living together would be a disaster and I'm pretty sure Frank didn't like it any more than I did. When he berated me for putting a salad fork in with the dinner forks, it was the beginning of the end.

It worked, until it didn't. We were happy, until we weren't. We have gone, as they say, our separate ways.

INSULTS I HAVE
ENDURED

I came to Toronto in 1968 to do a make-up year in the English department so I could go to graduate school. I started getting involved in various extra-curricular causes, and one day found myself at a meeting of the Stop Spadina movement. The Metro government wanted to build a highway from the north of Toronto all the way downtown, destroying some residential neighbourhoods. A woman, older than I, was holding forth on various topics, and I engaged in some back and forth with her.

"I find your ideas very interesting," I said. "Can we get together for coffee some time? What's your time like this week?"

A man standing slightly behind her right shoulder, who I deduced was her husband, burst out laughing. "Oh, I don't think so," he said, but what I heard in his condescending laugh were these words: "Who do you think you are, you little nobody, that the great Jane Jacobs would spend a minute of her precious time with you?" Humiliated, I skulked back into the mass of people who I now saw were standing in a reverential circle around the Great Woman.

One year, sometime in the late sixties or early seventies, I sat under a tree and caught feminism. I caught it bad, like a raging illness. I was full of anger that my mother and her generation, talented and brilliant though they might have been, were told they could only be fulfilled as wives and mothers. One day in the Hart House café I was holding forth about marriage and motherhood being institutions for the oppression of women. I had the attention of the table, and of Jill Conway, at that time a professor of history at the University of Toronto, later president of Smith College. She quite calmly took issue with what I was saying, arguing that in other times and places it was instead liberating for women to get married—in Ireland, for example, where at that time young women and young men both had to stay at home well into their thirties.

She went on to give example after example, and I continued to counterattack, but it was clear that my arguments were less and less convincing, and eventually I just sputtered out.

She had taken the X-Acto knife of her brain and sliced me up and laid me on the table like a pound of bacon.

Eventually I began to work on a doctorate in English at York University, studying, among other things, the plays of Bertolt Brecht. I heard there was a dance teacher giving classes in Toronto who had taught movement to the actors in the Berliner Ensemble, Bertolt Brecht's theatre in East Berlin. The Berliner Ensemble—the western world's epicenter of left-wing political theatre. The theatre of Kurt Weill and Lotte Lenya. I showed up at her class. Her name was Til Thiele, which I thought was a perfect Bauhaus name.

She was all of five feet tall, and rumoured to be seventy, or some said even eighty. She wore her thick black hair pulled back in a severe Euro-bun. She was very strict, and I sat at her feet, an adoring acolyte. Many innovators of modern dance focus on one part of the body. Martha Graham, for example, was all about the contraction, sucking in the torso and thrusting the arms and legs out, a kind of objective correlative of the philosophy of alienation around which her famous dances were created. For Til Thiele, the focus of movement was on the backside. "Motivate your movement from your backside," she said. "Make your backside a second face!" If it was good enough for Lotte Lenya ...

Once she asked us, "What is the word for the breathing out?"

"Exhalation," we answered.

"And the breathing in?"

"Inhalation!"

"Yes," she said. "When we were coaching Lotte Lenya for the scene in the *Threepenny Opera*, when she makes the famous scream, I taught her to scream on the inhalation, not the exhalation. This was the revolutionary way of movement."

How happy I was to sit at the feet of someone with insider information about the fabled Berliner Ensemble.

One day she called me up to the front of the class. You see this backside, she said, slapping my rear end. This backside is pudding. PUDDING! And she gave me another slap to demonstrate. Who was I to resent the critique of my ass by the great master?

A few weeks later I was at York University, sitting on the grass eating my lunch. It was a clear sunny September day, the sky that cerulean blue unique to southern Ontario in the fall. The architecture of York University is appallingly ugly, soul crushingly ugly. But the fine arts building there is an architectural jewel, with windows that start at ground level, tilt out, and soar thirty feet. I loved to watch the dance students doing their combinations, stretching, leaping and, in some cases, making their backsides a second face. I looked up and who should be striding towards me but the diminutive figure of Til Thiele herself, each step motivated by her tiny backside. I stood up and greeted her. Even though I towered over her I felt small and awkward.

"I've come to give the classes," she said. "What are you doing here?"

"I teach a class on Thursdays."

"What do you teach?"

"A course on Shakespeare."

"Shakespeare?" she asked, not hiding her shock.

"Yes, Shakespeare."

"Well, I guess I should treat you with more respect from now on!"

Goddamn right, Til Thiele, goddamn right!

———

If I was at times patronized and insulted by older women when I was young, now that I am old I am sometimes patronized and insulted by younger women.

And younger men. Take "OK Boomer." Go ahead, take it. This is an insult meme that is going around social media these days, often accompanied by rageful rants against people my age. That we destroyed the economy and the planet, that we take their jobs and their housing, presumably by not dying soon enough. If a so-called boomer objects, the taunter just repeats, "OK Boomer." It's an insult that brooks no response. (Of course this is not a personal insult, but I am taking it for the team.)

So I'm responding now. Where do you think the civil rights movement came from? Feminism? Gay rights? The environmental movement itself? You are talking to a generation who stopped a war—the Viet Cong themselves said that they conquered the greatest imperial force on the earth because they had the help of war resisters and protestors in North America and Europe.

I too thought my parents' generation was square, bourgeois, and boring. Remember who said don't trust anyone over thirty, at least until we turned thirty. But then, when I started hanging around the Communist Party, I met older comrades who had led the big industrial strikes in Sudbury, in Abitibi. Men and women who fought in the Spanish Civil War, something I knew about only vaguely. In my parents' generation there is an entire history of resistance that was written out of the accounts of Canadian history I studied in school. I was gladdened to feel a sense of solidarity and respect for these elders, these tough old warhorses.

So listen up you Gen X, Y and Zedders—did Joan Baez destroy the planet? Did Noam Chomsky take anyone's job? Does Michael Moore cause recessions? I don't think so.

But here's one even more egregious. I was at a writer's workshop with my brother and we each had to give a pitch for our work. His was very witty, and a young woman of my acquaintance turned to me and said: "Your brother is really funny. And you," (looking thoughtful) "you are just plain adorable."

Adorable? Are you joking? I've been called many things in my life. I've been called sarcastic, argumentative, and too smart for my own good. My ass has been likened to pudding. But no insult has stung as much as adorable. Is Jane Fonda adorable? Gloria Steinem? Angela Davis?

Don't you dare adorable me, sweetheart.

BLUE SKY

I see it coming. I saw it coming. I see it coming, over and over.

I am swimming in Georgian Bay, on my back, looking up. Blue sky everywhere, unfathomable space. To swim, for me, is to have no pain and no fear, to move freely, without awkwardness, without clumsiness, without the constant flashes of pain in my body. When I swim, I am strong; I am young again.

I can't move an inch without screaming, I can't reach for a tissue, I can only lie on my back and read my phone, my lifeline, my only connection to my world when the other people on the trauma ward moan and mutter and yell. Apart from me, they seem mostly to be drunk guys who fell on their heads.

The hospital chaplain said, on the other side of this, your big, beautiful, rich life will be waiting for you. And please consider that this is also your big, beautiful, rich life, right now.

I see it coming.

I don't see the trauma ward, the dirty whiteboard on the wall opposite, the opiates, the flowers, the nurses who casually talk about another patient trying to spread his feces on them while they are moving him. While they are moving me, I look up. You mean I'm not the most high maintenance patient on this ward? They laugh. I don't see the nurse who will yell at me when I cry out in pain, "You didn't move properly, it's your fault!" I don't see the neurologist who sweeps in with his entourage early in the morning, when I am too groggy to ask any questions. "The winged Mercury descends," I say. No one laughs.

I see it coming. A black SUV Jeep, the one with the giant grille that looks like huge fangs, coming for me, coming to eat me alive. Later, having never noticed this car before, I see it everywhere. Black, with that grille.

I see it coming. I think of this car now as the Angel of Death.

After six days of seeing nothing in my field of vision but the dirty whiteboard on the inner-city trauma ward, the suburban rehab hospital feels like a country club. I can see green from my window, and eventually get outside to see the garden, first in a wheelchair, then with a walker.

But the pain is still horrific. One night when a tall Russian nurse is trying to move me, I burst into tears. "Stop crying! You broken! Everybody broken! Whole ward is broken! You not most broken, stop crying!" I had to start laughing. Everybody broken indeed.

A year later, a few glorious weeks of reprieve at the cottage. No medical appointments. No knee specialist, no orthodontic surgeon, no chiropractor, no ophthalmologist, no trauma therapist. Just swimming and sewing. I am making a textile piece, based on the three Abrahamic religions. One is an interpretation of the rose wheel window at Chartres; one is of the dome of the Blue Mosque in Istanbul; one is of the Temple Wall in Jerusalem. I am sewing lapis lazuli blue and amber organza on to tulle. Delicate work, requiring concentration and care.

It surprises me that I have made something beautiful.

When my back hurts from sewing I walk into the water, feel the first grasp of the cold, start to swim. Sure and strong, and then that moment of bliss when I turn on my back and look up at the sky.

The impact of the Angel of Death broke my neck. A centimeter up or down and I would have died. Three weeks in hospital, three months in a neck brace. No swimming that summer. I sat on the beach every day and looked at the water with an intense ache in my soul.

What they say is true, everything slows down. I was in the passenger seat, and my partner said, "Are you all right? I'm OK." "I hurt my neck," I said. "Is the car going to explode now?" "No." I thought well, isn't it lucky to be in a car accident with a guy who knows more about cars than the next 1.5 thousand random strangers. He walked around but couldn't get my door open. Someone passed me, through the driver's side, one of those neck pillows people take on planes. I wondered who would have that in their car. Someone opened my door, a firefighter. "Here," he said. "I've got something better than that for you." He put a bright yellow and orange brace on my neck. I looked up at his face. Lined, not a young man. A face that had seen a great deal. His eyes radiated a pure and simple kindness. "We're going to put you on a stretcher now," he said, in his calm voice, "and get you to a hospital."

I see his face, over and over. Swimming on my back in Georgian Bay, I look up and see his face, as big as the sky.

I have come to see this man as the Angel of Mercy.

I keep thinking, I should try and find him and thank him. He probably saved my life.

Now, on the other side of it all, my big, beautiful rich life indeed awaits me, but it is different. I am different. The doctors gave me painkillers and instructions. The alternative practitioners I encountered gave me love and a truer healing, taught me how to calm my central nervous system, how to live with trauma, as I have learned how to live with loss. I still see it coming, feel the impact. But it's a part of me now, of who I am.

Whenever I swim, I look up into that blue infinity. This is what death is like, I think, just to dissolve myself into that space, to merge all the atoms of my body with the sky. Maybe the two Angels—the Angel of Death and the Angel of Mercy—have taught me, in the end, not to be afraid of death; to think of my end as a beginning. A big, beautiful, rich beginning.

FOOD

I suppose prison food is worse than hospital food, but it's hard to fathom that. I spent three weeks in the hospital five years ago, first on the trauma ward at St. Michael's, and then at St. John's rehab in North York. Compared to the downtown inner city St. Mike's, St. John's with its beautiful gardens felt like a pastoral retreat, if you could look past the bandaged, burned, and limping patients.

The food, however, was no improvement. The meat was stringy and drowning in a muddy brown liquid; there were mashed potatoes every lunch and dinner, and a kind of neon orange sludge for the *soi disant* dessert. The vegetables had lost any association with the real thing. One of my rehab occupational buddies was convinced that there was a giant mashed potato extruder in the basement, and the mush came up on an assembly line. "Oh look, fried snarf" I was heard to say more than once. A few old timers who came to visit remembered when they had real chefs there, and a menu, and you could choose your courses. This was not helpful.

One day two friends came to visit and brought food and drink. Divine mushroom crepes, real vegetables, delicious pasta, whitefish not actually boiled out of existence. I ate with a kind of ecstasy. And they had snuck in a bottle of champagne. Because of the neck brace I was forced to wear for three months I couldn't tilt the flute up to my lips to sip the champers. I almost cried, until my friend got a Styrofoam cup and I was able to drink. Despite the cocktail of painkillers I was on, including morphine, I imbibed with utter insouciance.

I remembered what I had to look forward to.

VIVE LA RÉSISTANCE!

After a long rehabilitation from a knee replacement, I was finally able to travel again. In the fall of 2017, I went on a river cruise on the Danube. I discovered, to my horror, that three quarters of my fellow passengers were Donald Trump supporters from Tennessee. I was travelling alone, and selected different dinner companions each evening. The conversations curdled my blood. "Ahm in a min-or-i-ty," drawled a young woman. "Mr. Trump is mah pres-i-dent. Whatever you read about him is all lahs. Jes' lahs!" The Democrats I met practically fell into my arms when they found out I was Canadian. Will you sponsor us? they only half-jokingly asked.

During the days I sometimes left the tours and set out on my own. In Prague I spent an afternoon in Dox, the city's contemporary art gallery. I entered a room with a very large photograph on the far wall, full of glorious rich colours—saffron, vermilion, emerald, azure. Coming up close to the image I realized it was a photograph of small groups of families in brightly coloured clothes, standing in a field. The wall text said they were Kurds who had to abandon their village when it was attacked by American soldiers. A few hours after this photo was taken, they had to return to their bombed-out village for fear of reprisals from the Iraqi army. "For the Kurds," the text concluded, "simply to be happy is an act of resistance." Is it true for all of us, I wondered. Is happiness an act of resistance?

Six months later, in the spring of 2018, I was in Europe again, this time in London, for the first time in ten years. Doug Ford, a right-wing populist who models himself on his hero, Donald Trump, had just been elected Premier of Ontario, my province. Brother of the late, notorious Rob Ford, the crack-smoking mayor of Toronto, Doug was quickly on his way to slashing the new sex education curriculum, cutting funds for the care of autistic children, cutting school budgets, cutting health care and environmental protections, such as they were, and so on. Depressed and angry, I wandered around the Tate Modern for a few hours, hoping to come upon the Mark Rothko room. I had seen those paintings the first time I went to the Tate, ten years earlier. At that time, sitting on a banquette in the middle of the gallery, I slowly turned 360 degrees, looking at the paintings. Then I burst into tears, sobbing, oblivious to my surroundings, not caring what anyone thought.

Mark Rothko was a colour field painter who died by suicide in 1970. Of all modern painters, his works are the least effective in reproduction. They are simply veils of colour, often only two or three colours in each painting. Their luminosity can't be conveyed in any way other than by seeing them in the flesh. Originally meant for a restaurant installation, he pulled the paintings and donated them to the Tate Modern, where they have a room to themselves.

I wondered what effect the paintings would have on me now. I finally found the room, sat down on that same banquette, looked at the paintings and started to cry. I cried really hard, for a good five minutes, without knowing why, and, oddly, without feeling sad.

It's taken me a long time to find the words to describe that experience. It was as if a space opened up, a space of lightness and no boundaries, a space of eternity that was nonetheless here and now. A space of tenderness and grace, of possibility and human kindness.

I have had, for the past fifteen years, an extremely ambivalent relationship to Christianity. I go to church each week, and the liturgy of the Church of England brings me solace, and taking communion does, indeed, bring me into communion with what I'll call the divine, and with the community of faith. A friend asked me once why, then, was I ambivalent, and I said, well there are three reasons. The first reason is colonialism. The second: colonialism. And the third ...

And, of course it's more than that, it's the just plain dumb weirdness of some of the Bible stories, the talents and the slave owners, the circumcision covenant, and the manna in the desert. I don't know if I believe the miracles happened, I don't know if I believe in the divine birth, I don't know if I believe in the resurrection. I often find Jesus, the man depicted in the Gospels, to be opaque and arrogant. I'm not convinced that there was a historical man named Jesus. Yet I think these things are also more than myth, more than metaphor, more than literature. So, I flail around, not really knowing what I believe. But when I search for a way to describe that space that opened up to me—twice, ten years apart—looking at paintings by Mark Rothko, I think of one word: Christ.

Another thing happened when I was in that space, both in the room and in my psyche. I saw Donald Trump and Doug Ford—and all the other demagogues the Empire has thrown at us down the centuries—as receding figures, as if I was seeing them through the wrong end of a telescope. How little they looked, how puny, how insignificant! In this inviolate space, created both in the room and in the contemplation of it in the months that followed, I began to understand that inhabiting it is a way to resist tyranny, in the same way that mocking diminishes tyranny's power. I had a glimpse of what martyrdom might be about, a way of being that is so grand, so full of compassion and mercy as to be unassailable, even in death. That death itself cannot vanquish this space.

I've begun to think about what resistance means in a world growing daily darker and darker. To have hope when all about us prompts despair. To stop obsessing about the news, reading only the headlines to stay minimally informed. Whenever I catch myself feeling compulsively angry, or afraid to the point of paralysis, I make a conscious effort to interrupt myself, to try and find again the feelings evoked by Mark Rothko's paintings. Courage is resistance. Creating beauty is resistance. Seeking beauty is resistance. Making common cause with everyone who is organizing, protesting, struggling, mocking, bearing witness and taking risks.

I think those smiling Kurds in their bright clothes were in this space. The artists who drew and painted in the Nazi camps.

Most of us are not, of course, Kurds. Most of us are privileged Canadians, more so if we are straight, white, male, or any combination. But every one of us is potentially under attack. Even as I write this, do you think the data Facebook is collecting isn't making its way to Homeland Security, to the RCMP, to ChatGPT?

But they can't touch the vision I had in the Mark Rothko room, a generative vision that leads out in so many directions, directions our resistance can take. Our happiness (albeit happiness tempered by our knowledge of privilege), is our very survival. As the actual space of Jerusalem and Palestine explodes, severing limb from limb, let us create the new Jerusalem, understanding that justice is beauty, that compassion is our most powerful weapon, that joy is at once our most effective line of defence and our first and best line of attack.

POSTSCRIPT

Here's some things Rothko said about his own work:

My paintings' surfaces are expansive and push outward in all directions, or their surfaces contract and rush inward in all directions. Between these two poles, you can find everything I want to say.
  —(https://en.wikipedia.org/wiki/Mark_Rothko)

I am interested only in expressing basic human emotions—tragedy, ecstasy, doom, and so on. And the fact that a lot of people break down and cry when confronted with my pictures shows that I can communicate those basic human emotions ... The people who weep before my pictures are having the same religious experience I had when I painted them. And if you, as you say, are moved only by their color relationship, then you miss the point."
  —(Cited in James Elkins, *Painting and Tears*, p. 12–13)

People weeping in front of Rothko paintings is a common occurrence, as can be seen from messages left in the visitors' books at the Rothko Chapel in Houston, Texas.

Then there's Stendhal Syndrome. It was named by a psychiatrist, Graziella Magherini, who wrote a book about "hysterical tourism"— people who weep, sweat, swoon, suffer from vertigo, or vomit in front of paintings. "She prescribes tranquilizers and advises bed rest, and she reports that most people recover as soon as they have spent some time away from the artworks."
—(Elkins, p. 45)

NOSY NEIGHBOUR

In my back yard, a beam of light shines out of the dark night sky. My neighbour, with her flashlight again, snooping. What is it this time? We both park our cars in the laneway, a situation leading inexorably to tensions. Or perhaps it's the return of the dreaded downspout debacle: did I forget to turn on the switch that warms the downspout, which melts the snow, which keeps the water out of our adjoining basements?

Or perhaps it's the cat.

You might think that the greatest culture war is pro-life versus pro-choice, or Mac vs. Windows, but really, it's whether or not you let your cats go outside. "Would you let a two-year-old go outside and play on the road?" a shocked friend once asked. But Buxtehude is a barn cat, despite his highfalutin' name, born to prowl. If I don't let him out he claws the baseboards to shreds. My neighbour disapproves. Sometimes her obsession is about Buxte himself—will he freeze, starve, or die of thirst if he stays out all night or occasionally, in warm weather, for a couple of days? At other times, it's about his potential and actual victims: mice, chipmunks, birds. The day he actually caught a bird, the whole neighbourhood was in an apoplectic frenzy.

I should be more understanding, less judgemental. My neighbour was forced into early retirement from a demanding and prestigious job, and all that acumen and drive and energy now goes into our parking situation, our shared downspout, and the accursed cat. She once asked for a key, so she could let the cat in if I was away. This was in the early days, before tensions escalated, and it seemed like a good idea. Then came a few years when she would open my front door to let the cat in, even if I was sitting right there in the living room. Almost every day. I finally asked for the key back, and she was distraught beyond measure. Now she's out there in the dark, shining her damned flashlight, prowling, prying, snooping.

I always seem to screw up some little thing and she always discovers it. The time I told my brother, who had been staying, to leave his key under the blue bin in the front yard, and promptly forgot all about it. Did I imagine a subtle note of triumph in her voice, in her shocked tone, when she told me she'd found my key? The time she emailed me to ask if she could park closer to the invisible dividing line, and I wrote back and said sure, I'll move the car. But as she ever so slyly pointed out, I was up in Thornhill and the car of course was with me.

We live in Victorian row houses, six of them altogether, and another neighbour arranged for us all to have our eaves cleaned after the leaves were down. Walking out to the car I saw the eaves cleaner van in her parking space, and her back gate open. I ran up to the man on the ladder beside her house and told him I would leave my gate open so he could clean my eaves. Of course, she was watching, and called out triumphantly, "It's only October, they won't come until November when all the leaves are down. He's just fixing one of my eaves. You'll get an email when they're coming to do all of our houses."

Doh!

To have a nosy neighbour is to live in a state of continuous low-level resentment. I need to be more compassionate, for both our sakes. She lost her job, and her husband died. I could be a better person. I must become a better person.

After her husband died I asked her in and we had a glass of brandy together. I talked about my own grief, trying to find a way to be kind, to be sympathetic, but she seemed oddly disconnected.

I went away for four or five days and when I came back my niece, who had stayed to house-sit and look after the cat, said the neighbour knocked on the door every day to let the cat in. "I was afraid he'd be out there in the cold," my neighbour said, "that he would go for days without water."

Maybe I should just give her the damned cat and be done with it!

There's no end to this story, because nosy neighbours don't stop being nosy, and don't stop being neighbours, unless one of us moves or dies. And I don't stop being forgetful about eaves and cars and cats and keys.

And I still just keep on trying, and just keep on failing, to be a better person.

DADDY'S MONEY

Society's final taboo is money. People would rather hang their bare ass out of a car window than disclose their income. Especially if that income is high. You can talk about religion, you can talk about sex, you can talk about politics—no matter how contentious. But you cannot talk about money. Especially if you have a lot of it.

There are only two ways an artist today can manage to find the time to make art. The first is to teach, which leaves two to five months a year for art. It used to be that art schools would hire artists to teach drawing, painting, and sculpture. But increasingly, as art schools such as the Nova Scotia College of Art and Design, Emily Carr University and the Ontario College of Art and Design University (yes, that's what it's called) become degree-granting institutions—which makes them eligible for significantly more government funding, not to mention bringing greatly enhanced prestige—one needs first an MFA and now a PhD to teach there. So that's six to ten years of post-secondary education, incurring a vast student debt, and then the usual story of hen's teeth vacancies, and people with PhDs taking low-paid, unpredictable sessional jobs. Even as an elementary or high school teacher (two months a year instead of five for art-making), jobs are scarce and art programs are being viciously cut.

The second is to be married or in a stable long-term partnership with someone with a professional or better income. A doctor, lawyer, accountant, academic—someone who thinks there's a certain cachet in having an artist for a partner, or who may genuinely believe in their work and want to support it. This arrangement is fraught. Being financially dependent on a partner can be infantilizing; one may lose one's self-respect; one may always feel one-down in decision making; there is inevitable resentment on both sides.

The fates issued me another kind of ticket: daddy's money. My father, who grew up in the Jewish ghetto of Montreal, was born with a Midas touch and a seemingly bottomless fount of irrepressible and irresistible charm. During the Depression, he gathered a team of young women and took them through the Maritimes selling magazines. My mother was chief among them, and they married in Moncton, New Brunswick, in 1936. They lived well during those difficult times. I remember a friend of my mother's telling me, "She just took the rest of the uneaten pork chops and threw them in the garbage. I never saw anything like that in my whole life!" People were poor, but in Canada, none were as poor as farmers in the Maritimes, yet they couldn't wait to shell out money for magazines sold by my charming father. After the war, on a veteran's grant, he bought a peat moss bog on Lulu Island (now Richmond, B.C.) and settled down to raising a family and a fortune.

As a child and teenager, although it was anything but a happy household, no material want was stinted. I wanted to skate, I got white buckskin figure skates, the envy of every eight-year-old girl at the skating rink. The best new bicycle; the best outfits. By the time I was in my twenties, my father was, in a word, rich. One of his favourite adages (he had many) was that he didn't believe children should have to wait until their parents died for their inheritance. He gave me shares in many of his companies. These shares declared dividends. These shares were eventually sold.

His greatest pride and joy was a commercial golf course he designed and built in Richmond. Which, of course, I had shares in. When he sold it, in 1990, I never had to work again.

At first I felt enormous guilt, and wanted to give the money away. Having that kind of wealth just didn't jibe with my egalitarian, Marxist political principles. My partner at the time, Terry, was gently dissuasive. "You have what everyone wants," he said. "Make use of it." Other friends were not so gentle: are you out of your fucking mind? was the general feeling. So I found an "ethical" investment advisor, who has made it possible, for the last thirty years, for me to make art, live in a beautiful house, travel to over fifty countries, and spend summers in a cottage on Georgian Bay. I say "ethical" in quotation marks because capital and the income it generates, even when ethical screens are applied for fair labour and sound environmental practices, and for avoiding tobacco, are never more than three or four steps away from child and forced labour, from environmental degradation, from the basest, most abject suffering on the planet.

I have spent my whole adult life convinced of the rapacity, the evil, of capitalism. And I have spent my whole adult life benefitting from it. Hypocrisy, thy name is Robin.

With so many young people, and indeed some not-so-young people, living paycheque to paycheque, the gap between the rich, like me, and the poor is sinful. How can I, in all conscience, espouse a social Gospel? People like me, and people far wealthier than me, should be taxed more. Jeff Bezos could feed millions on a fraction of his zillions. But the system itself needs to be overhauled, needs to be replaced by an economy based not on untrammeled, greedy profiteering, but on caring for everyone equally, and for the planet too.

But in the meantime, if I'm honest, I'm not willing to give up my freedom.

I'm always bemused when people congratulate me on the work I do (although increasingly it's more surprise that someone my age is still at it), because I sit on a veritable mountain of privilege. I'm white, cis-gendered, educated. Except for a year or two in my early thirties, I've never had a single minute of financial worry or stress. And because there's a generation between me and the source of the money, none of the friction, none of the resentment that exists when one is supported by a partner or spouse. For all his many faults—and his crimes against my gender—my father never expected anything in return for his immense generosity.

Still and all, a mixed blessing of sorts. I never had to learn the hard lessons of being an adult. I could lip off to a boss, get fired, and not care (it happened more than once). Headstrong, emotional, and capricious, maturity came very late in the day for me. I think if I hadn't had daddy's money, I would have soon learned, perforce, in any workplace, to rein in my unruly nature. Fortunately, making art saved me from myself, gave me a purpose in life and a structure to my days. I learned to be disciplined, not procrastinate, meet deadlines.

I've husbanded my money well. Although I probably spend more on restaurant food and travel than most, I'm not extravagant. And now that most of my friends are retired, at least for the ones who have pensions—and many have received sizable inheritances too—there's not much difference in the way we live our lives. Retirement has given them the priceless gift I've had for thirty years: time.

"You don't know how it feels, to struggle, to be broke, to worry about bills, food on the table," I've been told more than once, and that is true. Also true: It is easier for a camel to pass through the eye of a needle than for a rich woman to enter heaven. Also true: any guilt and ambivalence I might have is matched by my most profound gratitude.

I MARRIED MY WORK

I slow my steps as I walk past a Dixieland band playing "Here Comes the Bride." I'm wearing a dress made out of hundreds of pages torn out of old work books—to-do lists, meeting notes, phone numbers. Forty-three notebooks in all, which I've saved for forty years. The dress has a ten-foot train, carried by my two stunningly handsome step-grandsons, nineteen and fifteen years old. Ahead of me walks my fourteen-year-old step-granddaughter, handing out long-stemmed roses, also sculpted and folded out of book pages. On my head is a turban, inspired by Vermeer's *Girl with a Pearl Earring*, twisted into a rosebud shape at the crown, with an attachment at the back constructed of collaged papers from my book pages and mirroring the shape of the train. I carry a bouquet, also made of book pages.

This performance is called "I Married My Work," September 12, 2020, in Christie Pits Park in Toronto. At the end, I turn my back to the wedding guests and toss my bouquet. A close friend catches it.

The Dixieland band was pure serendipity—they happened to be jamming in the park and offered to play *Here Comes the Bride* when they saw me.

Two days later, I ask my partner, "Did it feel sad for you that I declared to the world that I married my work, and I didn't marry you?" He admitted, with surprising frankness, it did indeed upset him. He said someone at the event asked him, "Always an usher, never the groom?" I laughed. He didn't.

The event was so joyous for me, and in the midst of the pandemic everyone was so happy to be outdoors, masked and distanced, of course, but outdoors, chatting with friends, just like at an art opening or a theatre first night. I felt like a queen.

But I also felt, and still do, a sense of poignancy, of bittersweetness. When I first started keeping those notebooks, in the early days of the second wave of feminism, I knew I would never be an artist's wife; what I wanted, without having a clue how to go about it, was to be The Artist. But who would be my wife? Because the truth is, as every successful male artist will tell you, every artist must have a wife. Or wives.. Someone willing to make the sacrifices necessary for the artist to create. Someone to bring the tea in bed in the morning, to bring home the paycheck, to hold the hand, to soothe the brow, to vacuum the rug.

Because being an artist, if you're worth the name, is to be an artist every waking moment, whether or not you're making work. You are always making work in your unconscious, you are always creating, with or without your allegedly requisite ten thousand hours. And on some level, you don't care who pays. To be an artist is to be profoundly selfish. To care more about the work than about anything or anyone else.

Everyone who has loved me, and whom I have loved, has paid a price. My family, my lovers, and most especially, my daughter. It was not right to sacrifice a child on the altar of my artistic obsession, but I did. I regret it more than anything else, and God knows I have a lot to regret. But I don't think I could have, or would have, changed it. I read accounts of women writers and artists who surrendered their creativity to raise their children, and then resumed it. But even though, when my daughter was young and most in need of my undistracted love, I had nothing to show for it, I knew that if I stopped at least trying, I would stop altogether. I knew if I renounced the desire to create I would renounce myself, and that I would die a spiritual, if not an actual, death. I told myself—lied to myself, perhaps—it was more important for my daughter to see her mother fulfilling her dreams than to be reading her endless stories or playing endless boring games while she smouldered with resentment. But that's not true. It's more important for children to have their parent's love and attention all the time.

After my husband died in 2003, I often went into the little storage room at the back of my storefront studio, which I had turned into a meditation room, and pounded on a drum and howled. I often wondered what the patrons of the adjoining Portuguese sports bar thought of that. Yet the years following Terry's death were the most productive of my life. In one year, 2010, I did three major art installations and performances. Grief propelled me, and art made it possible to survive grief.

What makes me do it? Why do I have to make art? Sometimes I think that, because I've had financial independence, I have to justify my existence, to myself and to the world. But mostly, ideas come unbidden to my consciousness, from somewhere in the ether, and I feel compelled to manifest them.

Does anyone ask a male artist if he has regrets? If he was selfish? If he sacrificed his children, friends? When I look at the self-portraits Rembrandt painted when he was old, I believe he did ask these questions of himself. But his honesty is rare. I'm no Rembrandt, and I don't know, and possibly don't care, if my work will outlast me. I hope it creates some memories, happy, poignant, and thoughtful, as I think it did that Saturday in Christie Pits, on a September afternoon during COVID-19, for those who came to watch my wedding procession. It brought people together, as I hope other projects of mine have done.

For what is art for, if not to bind our hearts together?

THEY ALSO SERVE
WHO ONLY SLEEP
AND DREAM

We're sitting drinking coffee at the White Spot restaurant in the Oakridge shopping mall in Vancouver. I remember well going with my parents to the first White Spot, on Granville Street, because it had a Treasure Chest, and any child could open it and pull out a wrapped present, usually a toy or a puzzle. But this White Spot is just a generic café, with the same bland walls, boring "art" and plastic chairs found, I'm sure, in every shopping mall in North America. We were mostly thoughtful and didn't speak much; John McLean was someone I could always be comfortably silent with.

We were at the White Spot to have a conversation about death. His death. We had just come from photographing him holding a golf club at the Langara Golf Course, with a profusion of colourful flower beds in the background. Then I photographed the scene without him in it.

John was one of seventy participants in an art project I did in 2018–2019 called *Missing You*. I invited each of them to let me photograph them in a place they loved, a place that had meaning for them, and then photograph that place without them in it. I sent them a series of questions I wanted to ask them about their own mortality; then I taped their responses:

> Do you think about what happens to us after we die, and
> if so, what are your thoughts?

What would you like done with your mortal remains?
Do you sometimes imagine a funeral, a celebration of life,
    a memorial?
Are you afraid of dying?
What do you hope your legacy will be?
What music do you want your mourners to hear? If there is
    one piece of music you had to choose, what would it be?

John's responses were edited for the final video:

Both my parents were cremated and both of them are in
my living room now. I have a big Chinese urn and they're
in bags in there. I'll go in there with them.

I'm eighty, that's enough. All the guys I know that play
basketball, they've all got stents.

I've written a lot of obituaries, at least one became quite
famous. And there was a guy who liked them, and he said
what do I have to do to get you to do my obituary, and I
said, you gotta die.

Neither of us mentioned, there in the White Spot, that he had prostate cancer.

John McLean was a close friend of my older brother for over seventy
years, and I had known him almost that long. When I heard, six
months after that conversation, that his prostate cancer was terminal, that he'd only been given three months to live, I flew out to
Vancouver to say goodbye. My brother and I went to see him in the
hospital twice, all three of us laughing and remembering old times.

When I went to kiss him goodbye, he said, "I won't forget you."
I said, "I won't ever forget you." Those were the last words
we spoke.

He was a humble man, a kind and loyal friend to my brother
and to our whole crazy, tragic family. He was the perfect Fifth
Business: I learned that he was the best man at five weddings. Smart

and witty, he was the epitome of loyalty, never straying from his devotion to my brother. They had a third friend, Bobby Donaldson. John McLean and Bobby played basketball together for decades, starting at Magee High School in Vancouver. My brother was known as Sonny; John McLean was Jinx, and Bobby, who grew up in a Baptist family and wasn't allowed to go to movies or dances, was oddly nicknamed Apeshit. These names, and their friendship, endured into their eighties.

John was a part of my life, albeit often incidentally, from when I was about seven, when he started coming to our house and letting me "shag" basketballs for him and my brother at the basketball net over the garage. That net was the epicenter of our street, Cypress Street. He spoke at my mother's memorial service in 1984. My mother was, to him, a very forward-thinking and progressive woman who introduced him to new ideas and ways of thinking—this was in the 1950s. A radical Marxist feminist in my youth (and mostly still today), I hadn't thought that my parents' progressive ideas were unusual, or realized that they had influenced me as well as John, and my brother and sister. But "Mrs. Bell," as John called my mother, had opened up a world to him when he was a young teenager.

On Sundays I attend services at Holy Trinity Anglican Church in Thornhill. Shortly after the lockdown, the church put its services on Zoom. Those first few weeks I found it quite alienating, and wondered if I would ever approach the communion rail and take the body and the blood again—the heart and soul of the Anglican liturgy. Easter seemed like a non-event, even though every year I have some kind of spiritual experience, something to convince me that the good will prevail, that light will drive out darkness, that life will renew itself. It didn't seem like that would happen this year. Zoom and spiritual enlightenment do not marry well.

I kept noticing that so many people I knew on social media were reporting intense dreams, often nightmares. I seldom remember dreams and had not had any that I remembered since the lock-down began.

But sometime during the night of Good Friday, I dreamt that I had to renew my driver's licence and do a driving test. A woman got into the passenger seat and told me she was the examiner. But first, she told me to drive up to the top floor of a high rise—there was a circular ramp like they have in parking lots—and I drove and drove and drove, up and up and up, around and around and around, in complete darkness.

"Turn here," she said. "Now you have to get onto the on-ramp of the Burrard Street Bridge." Suddenly we're in Vancouver. It was still dark, but with a very faint glow of light, just enough for me to see the dark grey concrete surrounding me on either side. It was the bleakest, most forbidding sight, claustrophobic and brutal like thirties Bauhaus architecture. I woke up and assured myself that it was a dream, shut my eyes and was immediately back in the car, driving in the dark. This happened two or three more times, and each time I watched myself watching myself dreaming one of the most frightening dreams I can remember ever having. At 6 am, I woke up and told my partner Frank how scared I was. He held my hand until I could drift off to sleep, and mercifully the dream finally ended.

I woke up feeling depressed and out of sorts. Midway through the morning I got an email from my brother telling me that John McLean had died in his sleep, in the early hours of the morning.

I realized that the dream I had coincided with the time of his death, three hours earlier in Vancouver. Was he terrified of dying, I wondered, and I had somehow picked that up? Or was it that I took on the fear and experienced it for him? The more I pondered this the more real that felt to me. That in experiencing his fear, I freed him to go to his death peacefully. I've had other occasions when I've felt like I've taken on someone's pain, telepathically, or intra-psychically, or something strange like that.

I told my Anglican friend Mary about all of this, feeling slightly nervous that she would think I was woo-woo.

"No no, that's a thing," she said. "There's an opera called the *Dialogues of the Carmelites*, which takes place during the French Revolution when monks and nuns were killed if they didn't renounce their faith. One young nun is terrified of dying and fears she will capitulate. The Mother Superior of her order dies an agonizing and terror-filled death. The implication is that it is the wrong death, that she has died someone else's death, that she has taken on the fear of the young nun, who then goes to her martyrdom with serenity." So there's a precedent, at least in the imagination of the opera's writer and composer, Francis Poulenc.

Late on Easter Sunday night, after this conversation with Mary, I watched a taped Easter service that began in utter darkness. Slowly, slowly, a flame became visible, which I inferred was in a small bowl on a table. The Priest lit the Paschal candle from this flame, and the Resurrection came again, as it comes every year. The terror of the dream gradually faded away.

From the first time I met him, when I was seven, until the last time I saw him, John McLean always called me Sparrow.

I'D REALLY LIKE TO MEET JESUS CHRIST

Remember that old game people played at dinner parties—if you could meet anyone from the past, who would it be, and what would you ask them?

I'd really like to meet Jesus Christ. I'd like to ask him why he said the poor will always be with us. It's a really depressing thought, and I hate that he might be right, because I always believed that we could perfect the world, that we could bring justice. As his Jewish mentors and rabbis would surely have told him.

Plus, what's with eating with the tax collectors? I know that love thy enemy routine, but come on, those guys were evil, they collaborated with the Romans.

Then there are those interminable parables. Face it, some of them just don't make any sense whatsoever. I feel for the poor clergy having to preach about them, to try and explain them to a doubting, often bored, congregation. Frankly some of them just seem nonsensical to me.

And I'd like to ask what's with the miracles. I actually don't mind them as narratives, narratives of healing and abundance and transcendence. And I don't think of them as metaphors, or literature—there's something much more profound going on there. But what? That's what I'd like to ask. Virgin birth for starters; loaves and fishes, raising up the dead, driving the pigs into the sea. I don't think pigs would voluntarily run into the sea. Walking on water. And so on.

Lastly but perhaps most importantly, I want to know if he had sex with Mary Magdalene. She wasn't a prostitute apparently. That was a lie perpetrated by the early church fathers to discredit a woman who was the first person Jesus appeared to after he came back from the dead. Coming back to life after three days? I'd like to ask about that one too.

I have many questions, for a man who has a lot to answer for.

THE PANDO

He hands me the magic drink—single malt scotch, my daily liturgical five o'clock tittle. He has his own liturgical rum and coke. He sits on the couch, and I put my legs up on his lap, and we talk about whatever mundane things have happened in our respective days. I paid my bills; he sold something on Kijiji. Earlier we walked the dog. We have no plans for the evening, because we can't make any plans, can't do anything really, except for me, the endless round of novels and Netflix. I read compulsively, then with tired eyes, watch a series compulsively. Anything to numb the fear, the anxiety. My daughter lives in Los Angeles, where the positivity rate is 1 in 3. My 103-year-old mother-in-law is in a retirement home in Ancaster. Will the new variant rip through their lives, rip through mine? I've ordered N95 masks, $100 worth. No vaccines in sight, and now they're saying they might not be as effective as they thought. No end in sight. I sip my scotch. A pleasant tingly numb feeling goes through me, I lie back on the couch and have a 15-minute power nap. Such is the round of my days. Work, tasks, oblivion. There is nothing like falling deep down into a new series of episodes, unless it's falling into a few hours scrolling through Facebook. I think of Rilke, *Du mußt dein Leben ändern.* I must change my life. How? Give up alcohol? Find some more productive way of spending time? The hours stretch out, the pandemic stretches into the future, unknowable, uncertain, unconscionable.

So many odd memories come back during this pandemic. I've always loved merry-go-rounds, riding up and down in a graceful rhythm to a honkytonk tune. Once when my daughter was around four, we were visiting my brother in New York; I'd taken her to Central Park, and it was raining. I shook out my umbrella and lifted her up on the merry-go-round, thinking it would keep us out of the rain, if nothing else. She had a strange look on her face, as round and round she went, an otherworldly expression. Pumpkin, you have to get off, I said, it's time to go, we have to meet Uncle Johnnie, we can't be late. She ignored me, going round and round. I got more insistent; she got more resistant—a familiar pattern. Finally, I grabbed her and forcibly yanked her off her pretty horse. She screamed—no, she had a full-blown tantrum. So we were late anyway.

I still regret that I interrupted whatever transcendental experience she was having. To be a parent is to experience remorse; at least I never hit her. But maybe there are worse things.

Hard to know these days, what's a nightmare and what's reality. I'm having strange experiences when I sleep—I'm dreaming, but I'm also watching myself dreaming. And the feeling of dread and anxiety just continues what I feel in my waking state. And the dreams are so banal. I have to get to the airport to catch a plane for a conference where I am to present a paper, somewhere in Africa. I can't get to the airport, the taxi is late, the driver gets lost, charges me double. The airport is cavernous, I can't find the airline, can't find the gate, can't find the baggage check. The conference is to be about rocks, and I have a bag of rocks I'm taking with me, which, of course, I keep forgetting, losing, leaving behind. This dream, which my conscious mind was observing, dragged on and on. The rocks were so heavy, the plane was going to leave without me, I couldn't find a taxi to take me home, there wasn't any home anymore.

Sameness. I think that's the hardest thing for me about the plague. Everything is always and predictably and boringly the same, same, same. Nothing, and no one, and nowhere to look forward to. Day after day, get up, do some work, eat lunch, walk the dog, do some more work, exercise, have a drink, have dinner, watch Netflix.

Netflix, Netflix, Netflix. Occasionally a novel, any old novel, as long as it's escapist and doesn't make me think. Zoom this person, Zoom that person, this meeting, that meeting. Always the virtual image, never the real flesh and blood person.

On Sunday afternoon, I take a boredom nap, to try and get over my boredom headache. When I wake up, it's already 5:30 and we haven't walked the dog. We take her out, around the neighbourhood graveyard where I've walked her one million, three hundred and fifty thousand, six hundred and fifty-nine times. It's almost six, and it's still light out. I look at this light, this Ontario late winter twilight, this filtered, cold, austere late dusk, and the world, for a few moments, seems suddenly wondrous and beautiful again. I tell myself; we'll get through it.

And we do.

WHAT TO KEEP AND WHAT TO THROW AWAY

When it became clear that I, as a seventy-four-year-old woman, would have to isolate myself, and that my seventy-nine-year-old partner Frank would also have to lock himself down, I was in a quandary. We'd been together ten years, but had maintained separate domiciles, he in the suburb of Thornhill, me in my downtown Annex Victorian row house. I knew he would not, could not, come to my house—he hates being downtown, and can't function more than a few days away from his workshop. But, I moaned, what will I do in Thornhill? There's nothing for me to do here! Well, he said, what would you be doing at home? I had for years had the desire, if I ever had the time, to go through the contents of three large trunks in my basement, full of diaries, letters, and mementoes I'd saved over forty years. I had a couple of ideas for art projects I'd like to make out of it all. Well, he said, let's bring them up here.

Time was of the essence, as everything was rapidly shutting down. We filled eight giant extra-strength construction garbage bags and hauled them up to Thornhill.

For four weeks, in the first stage of the lockdown, I plunged into my past. Every day I spent a few hours reaching down into one of the giant bags and hauling up treasure. I never knew what my hand would bring up—old newspaper articles I wrote, old photographs, my daughter's baby clothes, sketch books, diaries, programs from all the plays I staged or acted in or directed. Sometimes the object brought back memories, but sometimes it was something I'd completely forgotten about and still can't remember. Two or three people, including Frank, looked at me sympathetically when I described this project, this dumpster dive through my previous lives. That must be very hard emotionally, was the consensus. It was the opposite. The exercise actually delighted me. For one thing, it's changed the narrative, the story I've told myself about my life.

I've always thought that except for my legs, which I've been quite vain about, I was very unattractive when I was a young woman. I remember my parents coming home from a wedding, I think it was a Ukrainian wedding, and all the women had to sit behind a curtain with their legs sticking out, and their husbands had to try and guess which one was their wife. "Of course, I knew your mother's legs right away," my father said. "They were the nicest, best ones." Which brings back another memory, walking in the University of Toronto quad in the late sixties, wearing a miniskirt. A group of boys followed me, whistling. Wow, great legs, they called out. I turned around—but look at the face, one cried, and they all made barfing sounds. Which simply confirmed my belief in my own ugliness. But when I look at the pictures another story unfolds entirely. I had long, thick, wavy, chestnut, hair; even, nicely proportioned features; pretty arched eyebrows; a fine nose; a sensuous mouth; and lovely soft eyes. I was a looker, all right, and it's shifting my psyche around to acknowledge it.

When I first started, in fits and starts, directing plays, writing plays, publishing poems and newspaper articles, I was thwacked each time by a hammer of shame. Reading over these pieces, I half consciously expected to feel that shame again, but it's not there—there's only the work. Some of it, to be sure, is substandard, but some of it is quite good writing, writing that stands up today. Similarly, I've told myself that since I learned how to draw for the first time in my late forties, I had no talent, that I survived as an artist on the strengths of my ideas. Looking through old sketch books, it's true that many of the drawings are stilted and awkward, but occasionally one will stand out as a pretty decent piece of work.

Each diary, each letter, each object, is a key that opens up a room in my psyche, one that may have been locked for decades. I pull up a piece of fabric. I'd saved a remnant from the kitchen curtains I'd had made for my house on Rushton Road, where I lived for over twenty years. The fabric is a print of Grandma Moses paintings, winsomely collaged together. I remember buying the cloth, how much pleasure it gave me, how I loved to look at those cheerful curtains in the mornings. And I remember my friend Barbara coming with me to look at the material, how delighted she was at how delighted I was, and that whole complex, now-ended friendship comes back in a rush of memories.

My diving into the past in this way is not chronological—a diary could be from thirty years ago, or ten years ago. It's like consciousness itself—our memories, which construct the narrative of our lives, are random, even chaotic. They are a pastiche, an assemblage of the past.

What to keep? My plan was to pare down three trunks to one. Some days I'm in a tossing out mood, and gleefully consign letters, old birthday cards, ephemera into the garbage bin beside my desk. Other days I'm attached to each object, can't bear to part with them, and put them in the various piles threatening to topple over and bury me.

Of what interest is any of this to anyone but me? What will happen to it all when I die? Do I want my daughter to read my diaries, some of which are pretty steamy writings about my sex life? Part of me wants to keep everything, part of me wants to just throw the whole enchilada in the trash.

It occurs to me that it's hardly accidental that I am going through this physical and psychical and emotional task in the middle of the coronavirus crisis. As we are repeatedly reminded, when we come out of this, the world will not be the same, there is no going back, any more than I can go back and relive the past that is housed in my three trunks. We also, collectively, and individually, must winnow out of this experience—what we want to keep, and what we want to throw away.

Pondering all of this, I take my single malt scotch outside at the end of the day, on one of the few days it's warm enough to sit outside. I look up, astonished. The world is clarified, the pale spring light outlines every branch, every new bud. I can see every striation in the bark of the old walnut tree at the back of Frank's yard. When I was in Grade Two, I got glasses for the first time, and suddenly I could read the blackboard, see the teacher's expression—it feels like that, as if I've just got a new pair of glasses. It's because we've stopped polluting the air, stopped driving, stopped travelling. The cars and planes are mostly gone; we've given the earth some space to breathe. The squirrels play in the yard; a raccoon sits in the crook of the big branch on that same walnut tree, and placidly looks down on us.

As the lockdown progresses, I start getting used to this simple life—less rushing around, less shopping, more time, more meaningful contact with friends, even if that contact is virtual. Let's not throw all of this away, let's at least keep some of it.

So I'm going to come out and say what even conservative journalists began hinting. What I do want to throw away is, in a word, capitalism. I want to trash a system that creates wealth for so few (myself included, privilege acknowledged), and misery and penury for so many. A system whose raison d'être is profit, which drives overconsumption and climate change. The journalist Ian Brown made the point that in other recessions or market downturns, the commentators were all male economists, sternly admonishing us to buy or sell, pull in our belts, or pull up our socks. In this plague, the experts are scientists, often female, and they are telling us to care for each other, to make sacrifices for the common good. And most people are doing so willingly, anti-maskers and anti-vaxxers notwithstanding. These are the things we must lovingly put back in our trunks when we at last are able to venture out of our houses.

MY COVID LISTICLE

Here I am, here again. The place I profoundly don't want to be. Another friend lies dying. A sweet man, a bon vivant, a beautiful classical pianist, a person whom no one ever said a bad word about. A gay man who lived his whole life with his sister and helped her raise her child. An ordinary extraordinary life, like all the rest of them. The eighth person I know who has died since Covid-19 began last March. None have died of Covid, but because of Covid, with one exception, none of us has been able to mourn together, to have a ceremony, a rite, to eat the funeral meats.

When I read *Antigone* in university, I couldn't understand it. She was forbidden by the cruel king Creon to conduct the traditional funeral rites for her brother. She defied Creon, and was put to death. It made no sense to me then, but oh, how I understand her now. It is a rift, a violent rip in the fabric of life, not to be able to come together to celebrate a life, to have that sensation, unique each time, that the whole person is greater than the sum of their parts. To commiserate with each person's unique community, to eat and drink and cry and laugh.

My brother's best friend, John McLean, died of prostate cancer. My brother and John's daughter and friends wanted to have a memorial at the basketball court where he played once a week up to his late seventies. Postponed indefinitely.

My friend Steve's dad Joe Horan, a feisty old trade union supporter and hydro worker, dedicated his life to looking after his frail wife Alice, who is now alone in a retirement home in Florida. Where Steve can't visit. A few friends gather outside and make a toast, but it's not the same. I want to meet his family, his cronies, I want to hear stories.

My brother-in-law David Shein was a schizophrenic who lived, along with his wife, on disability. He had a happy, stable, fifty-year marriage—unlike any of the other children in that family, and, God knows, unlike me, the serial monogamist. He died of lung cancer. But it was in the summer, and ten of us were able to go to a graveside service near the Hamilton Botanical Gardens. How blessed to see his family, who I've known for more than forty years. Even though the kind words on Facebook made my hackles rise, because people were not particularly kind to him in life, still, I understand the need to praise him, to offer up praise and gratitude for every single life.

And Joanna Chrystal, who survived breast cancer, bone cancer, brain cancer. Was a dragon boater. Climbed Kilimanjaro with her daughter, kayaked the rivers of the Yukon. Who, when told she had only two months to live, declared, "Time for a party!" And party we did, in High Park. She circled the road in a gold convertible Volkswagen Beetle, escorted by police and two of her dragon boat friends, towing a dragon boat. Each time she passed, we shouted with her, "Fuck Cancer!" She had the right idea, I think; have the funeral before you die. But her death, when it came not long after, was painful nonetheless, an absence, a disappearance.

Gerry McAuliffe, my late husband's brother, suffered from a rare genetic disorder called McArdle's disease that caused his muscles, periodically, to completely collapse. With a Grade Seven education, he became one of the top investigative journalists in Canada, sticking it to the mob for the *Globe and Mail*. And after nearly dying of his disorder several times, it was cancer that took him out. Fuck cancer. We had lost contact in the years after Terry died, but still, I grieved his death. Certainly, I would have attended his funeral, had there been one.

And my partner Frank's sister-in-law, Bobbie, one of the sweetest people I have ever had the privilege to know. She had been ill for many years, with multiple health problems, and had dementia, but always asked after me ("How's that lady friend of yours?" she asked Frank each time he called). My sorrow is more on Frank's behalf than my own. Bobbie got pregnant at eighteen, and Pete, Frank's brother, told her that he wasn't ready for that responsibility. She took the bus to Peace River in northern Alberta to be with her mother, and had the baby.

When Louise was a few days old, Pete had a change of heart, asked his parents to lend him the bus fare, walked into the hospital room and asked Bobbie to marry him. The origin story of their relationship told and retold down the years. They had two more children, and one of the happiest marriages I've known. He got a job as a firefighter, eventually becoming a fire chief. They bought farmland outside of Calgary where Pete raised cars and Bobbie made beautiful wreaths, created a beautiful garden, and filled the farmhouse with beautiful antiques.

Pete restores Packards and has a "Packard alley" on the farm, two rows of old cars he's eviscerated for parts. One of them has a tree growing out of the place where the engine once was. Every summer they hosted the Alberta Packard Club Family Picnic, which I, fish out of water, attended for several years. It's likely that next summer, assuming we've all been vaccinated, the Packard Club will have a memorial for Bobbie, whose hospitality they've enjoyed, and whose steaks, salads, and roast potatoes they've eaten, for forty years.

And now Douglas Freake, my old friend from the graduate English department at the University of Toronto. What an old boy's club that was! I remember running into Doug in Robarts library on my way to xerox the thirty-page bibliography for my thesis. "How many books did you read?" he asked, astonished. "About three hundred books and articles," I said. "And you?" "Well, I didn't read any, I just wrote about William Blake." Another one of those many moments when I realized it was different, then, being a woman. But I never minded Doug; we had an affectionate friendship. You couldn't be mad at him. He was just one of those people, a true mensch.

When I heard from our mutual friend Ken that they had taken him off life support (cirrhosis of the liver), I sat at the dinner table and finally wept—not just for Doug, but for all of them. Each death marks the death of a part of my past, the death of a part of me. Like it's being broken off, piece by piece by piece.

I stare at my wineglass, and have a violent, momentary desire to drink myself into oblivion. A glimpse of self-mutilation, self-annihilation, just to take the pain away, not to have to feel. I'm so sick of it. Sick to death of death. No anodyne sentiments here. I'm bored to death. I want to burn the whole goddamn house down.

It feels like a travesty to sum up a whole life in a few sentences, but sentences are all I have.

PLAY ON

I'm sitting on my palms, sweating. Telling myself over and over again, just breathe, breathe in two, three, four; hold two, three, four; breathe out two, three, four. When you get up there, remember to feel your feet on the floor, slow down, and *breathe* two, three, four. I wait an excruciating half hour, which seems like four hours.

Finally, my name is called, and I walk up to the stage, turn and bow to the audience, sit down on the bench. The keys loom up like giant yellowed teeth. The keyboard feels like it is three feet away from my hands, which instantly begin to shake. I forget to breathe. My hands, which appear to belong to someone else, start to play. I forget to slow down. I race through the piece, skulk off the stage. I have just finished a piano recital with forty children, all of whom acquit themselves very well indeed. Their generous parents and friends applaud me, but I know that once again I have undergone my twice-yearly exercise in abject humiliation. Every year for eighteen years and counting.

Why? I ask myself every June after the spring recital, every December after the Christmas recital. Why?

In the fall of 2002, two things happened. I had said to my partner Terry, for about six months, that I would like to take piano lessons, to really learn the Royal Conservatory of Music method. One day that September, signs appeared on each tree on my street: "I will teach you the RCM method in your own home." Then I got an email from a friend saying her daughter was selling her piano and did I know anyone who might be interested?

So the piano was bought and installed, and Milena Djordjevic-Gajic appeared on my doorstep, recently arrived from Belgrade with her husband and seven-year-old son. She was a successful concert pianist in Serbia, and her husband was a classical violinist, but they couldn't make a living there and they decided to come to Canada.

Her son Filip learned to play hockey, and rapidly learned English. Milena told me proudly that they were going to have a hockey game at his school where each child would skate out onto the centre of the darkened rink, a light would shine on them, and their name would be announced. *Les vrais canadiens.*

I had had a few years of piano lessons as a child, so I registered for the Grade Three RCM exam. In those early days Milena was very strict. "Count!" she yelled. "Slow down!" But she came with me to the exam, and the examiner was very sweet, and said how much they appreciated an "older student" learning to play. I got quite a good mark, but that was all just beginner's luck. After that, year after year the examiners were cold, haughty, and avoiding of eye contact. No matter how much I practiced, not just the pieces but scales, chord progressions, ear tests, I invariably choked at the exam, barely passing.

When I finally made it to Grade Eight, which was my goal, there were three examiners, sitting at a table on a raised platform, looking down on me. It was the nightmare vision of every Canadian child who was ever subjected to this annual exercise in mental torture. The fact that I was in my sixties didn't make it any less terrifying. I stumbled through the exam, and on my way out faced the three harpies and said, "That was it, my last exam, I'm never coming back." Sixty percent was the passing grade, and that is exactly what they gave me. I think they didn't want to see me again any more than I wanted to see them. I framed my certificate, and continued my piano lessons, becoming a fixture at Milena's twice-yearly recitals. Me and the forty children who don't choke.

In the hopes that I will one day play successfully, Milena gives me fairly easy pieces to learn, about a Grade Four or Five level. And

I plunk away most evenings, and somewhere along the line I did learn to count, and to slow down—something she tells her young students: "She finally listened to me, and you will too!" She often asks me to introduce the concert, welcome the parents, thank them for coming at the end.

Standing in front of a hundred people and speaking off the cuff holds not the slightest fear for me, so my piano performance anxiety has always been a mystery. Why do I do it? Milena herself has been a constant in my life for almost twenty years. She saw me through the terminal illness of my husband. After he died, I told her I had to stop taking lessons for a while, then I called her back a day or two later and signed up again. Something in the rhythm of our encounters, the stability of it, the knowledge that she would keep on yelling at me until I got the right tempo. And I saw her through the birth of her second child, and the death of her mother.

Somewhere along the line I accepted the cold fact that I simply don't have any musical ability, still less talent. In the visual arts, technique can be learned. People who say they can only draw stick figures are wrong—anyone can learn to draw. But you can't fake musical ability. You either have it or you don't, and I don't in spades. I come by it honestly. My father once had himself tested for his musical aptitude, and got a score of zero, that is, he was one hundred percent tone deaf.

But listening to music is another story. Everyone listens to music of one kind or another. I happen to like anything between about 1500 and 1850; I make an exception for Puccini, who composed *Madama Butterfly* in 1898 and died in 1924. I learned to love the Baroque repertoire from my friend Kent Biggar. I met Kent at a wild party, mostly gay men, sometime in the seventies, where I also met a man named Eugene, who was not gay. I was too drunk and stoned to drive home, so Kent said we could sleep at his apartment in Kensington Market, within walking distance. Eugene and I slept on the floor, and Kent slept in his bed on the second floor. In the morning he came down the open staircase clad in only his skin. Now Kent was slender, narrow of shoulders and hips. One part of his anatomy, however, was impressively large. I looked up and spoke my thought out loud: "My goodness, what a grievous loss for womankind!" I sent Eugene home, and Kent and I went for breakfast at the United Dairy.

Over a five-hour conversation a friendship was born that was to last thirty years. As a nineteen-year-old, he had a transcendingly exquisite voice, and was being groomed by the famous contralto Maureen Forrester and her circle to be the first great Canadian countertenor. He was witty and charming, and much taken up by the leading classical musicians of the day. Then he developed a rare bone disease that impacted his vocal chords, and he was suddenly dropped back into obscurity.

When he was a teenager his father threw him down the basement stairs when he realized his son was gay, and then kicked him out of the house, so he had no education beyond high school. He went to work at the Toronto Reference Library and taught himself to play the harpsichord, and later built his own instrument. He only played for himself, every day after work, and for a few chosen friends. I was one of those lucky ones.

Every few months, for years, Kent invited me over for dinner, and then sat down and played—Bach, Scarlatti, Vivaldi, Buxtehude. I sat in his beautifully decorated little apartment and heard that music as it was meant to be heard, in someone's living room. I can't say I could even explain counterpoint—I didn't learn that music so much as I imbibed it, inhaled it.

Most of Kent's friends and lovers died in the AIDS epidemic in the eighties. He once went to a dinner party with eight men, and two years later he was the only one still alive. "They should be studying me," he said more than once. He survived the virus, but he didn't survive the grief. He smoked too much and drank too much, and at the age of fifty-six died of lung cancer and bone cancer. There's a book to be written about men who walked so many of their loved ones to the grave and then, twenty years later, died of a broken heart.

I can close my eyes and hear those rich notes cascading all around me, like rain, like starlight, an aural tapestry, filling the room and me with baroque gorgeousness. Against all reason, I believe in an afterlife, because I believe that Kent's harpsichord playing cannot die, that my idea of heaven would be to sit in his living room and hear that music once again. Some lights simply can't be extinguished, or so I try to believe.

Kent was a musical snob, eschewing what he called "that modrun music" (he made an exception for Joni Mitchell), but he was always so generous with me. He taught me some Schubert songs and he would accompany me as I sang, probably off key. (I once belonged to a choir, and the choir mistress said to me, "I know if Robin gets it, everyone else will get it." I thought it was a compliment until I realized she meant if I could learn it anyone could.) But we both loved those sessions, and when I was learning how to be a theatre director, I adapted L.M. Montgomery's novel *Magic for Marigold* as a stage musical. I wrote lyrics and Kent composed the music. There was one song we especially loved to sing and play, a song about friendship, and about one friend dying.

I think about Kent whenever I listen to Bach, and whenever I sit down to play the piano. After all, talent doesn't matter. Only love does.

A couple of years ago, another older woman, even older than I, started taking lessons from Milena. She was eighty something, and still sang in a jazz band. Her playing was beautiful. She was just naturally musical. She was always very nice and friendly to me, but I, being the unevolved person that I am, experienced fits of jealousy whenever she played at a recital. I wanted to be the token older woman, who everyone thought was great just for trying. It didn't matter quite so much that I always screwed up, because everyone was kind, and also there was no basis for comparison. But Alice showed me up.

One day in the middle of a lesson, I confessed my jealousy to Milena. "She's going to be your favourite student," I said, "she's so much better than me, and I'm afraid you'll ask Alice to do the welcome and the thank you at the recitals." Milena looked at me with blank-faced astonishment. "Are you kidding," she said, "what are you, six years old? My youngest students are more mature than this!"

(Never one to pull her punches, that Milena.) Then she softened, "But you are my Robin," she said, "you've been here since the beginning!" Assuaged, I conquered my jealousy. And anyway, Alice moved to Calgary.

I go to the first lesson after Christmas. It's great to be back after the break, and we have a good lesson. As I'm leaving a small girl comes in with her mother. A very serious little girl with glasses. "Look at you," Milena says, "you've grown over Christmas!" "I'm seven now," the child replies, with a mixture of pride and shyness. All day I am consoled by the image of this sweet child. And by the thought of how good and kind our teacher is with her young students, and with unmusical me, the reigning queen of Milena Djordjevic Gajic's piano studio.

AND TO ALL A
GOOD NIGHT

My friend Kathleen asked if I'd like to go to a Christmas concert with her, a concert of offbeat Christmas songs. I trust her excellent judgement of popular culture, so I said sure, and we met for dinner at the Pearl, a good Chinese restaurant at Queens Quay on the waterfront. Stuffed with dumplings and other delicacies, we made our way over to the Harbourfront Theatre in the Power Plant building.

It was the *Art of Time Ensemble*'s annual Christmas concert. There was a ten-piece orchestra, and a single violin began by playing "Silent Night," a simple and pure version of the ubiquitous, time-worn carol. Then the orchestra joined in, one by one, and played a jazz version of it. While this was happening, the Canadian Opera Company's children's chorus filed in at the back of the stage, raised up about fifteen feet and dimly lit. Jackie Richardson, who by the end of the evening I would come to regard as Canada's national treasure, sang a powerful blues version, and Jessica Mitchell, a local singer who I hadn't known, came on stage and sang Tom Waits' "Christmas Card from a Hooker in Minneapolis." Then the Children's chorus sang "Silent Night," a cappella.

It was going to be a special night.

David Wall sang "(I'm Spending) Hanukkah in Santa Monica." Someone sang "Christmas in Prison," and someone sang "Christmas in Washington." Someone did a drunken version of a drunken Christmas song. David Wall talked about the most popular song ever written, by Irving Berlin, who like the authors of so many other classic modern carols, was a Jewish songwriter. Then he told us he'd had "I'm Dreaming of a White Christmas" translated into Yiddish, and he sang it in Yiddish and English.

Each time someone sang, I felt I was hearing the song for the first time.

But nowhere was this so startling as when Jackie Richardson sang "The Little Drummer Boy," a song I loathe, a song that epitomizes Christmas cheese piped into a shopping mall. She started with just the sound of an African drum, and slowly built up the song as the orchestra joined her. Her voice is like a rum-soaked cake, everything rich and warm and sweet and delicious. I heard her spiritual power, her ability to create a sacred space with each note. She built to a crescendo, and then a decrescendo, singing "parum pa pum pum" a cappella, softer, and softer, inviting the audience to join her, until it was just a whisper, and then there was silence. And in that silence, she said, "God bless you."

For the finale, the whole orchestra played, and all six of the singers came on stage and sang John Lennon's "Happy Xmas (War Is Over)" with its famous line, "War is over, if you want it, war is over now." The song ended, the instruments and the singers fell silent, and the children's choir sang one line, a cappella, as the lights dimmed. They sang, oh so softly and sweetly, "War is over now."

With hearts replete, we took the subway from Union Station; Kathleen got off at Wellesley, and I changed to the Bloor line and sat down beside a very tall, very thin young man. I realized that he was humming something, and, as one does, my first thought was perhaps he was mentally ill. Then I thought, maybe he's got earphones on. Neither of these was the case. I realized the tune was familiar, and it took me a few moments to recognize that he was humming the melody of "The Holly and the Ivy," one of my favourite carols. Very softly, I started humming it with him. He didn't really notice, he seemed to be in his own world. But when he started singing the words, I joined in, just loud enough that he could hear me. "But of all the trees that are in the wood, the holly bears the crown." I was facing forward, but I could see out of the corner of my eye that he was puzzled. I joined in just a tiny bit louder, and turned to him, and sang with him: "The rising of the sun, and the running of the deer, the playing of the merry organ, sweet singing in the choir." He looked at me in utter astonishment as he got up—"This is my stop. I wish I didn't have to get off here," he said. "Thank you, and merry Christmas!" he called out for the whole car to hear. "Merry Christmas to you," I answered, and continued on my journey home, as light as a feather, as soft as the softly falling snow.

DUSK

From the age of eleven until my mid-fifties, my interior life was cyclical. Every month had its own inner events and rhythms. There would be a few days, or if I was lucky, a week or even ten days, when I felt alert, attractive. My hair got shiny. The twin raptors of self-doubt and self-recrimination released their talons from my neck. I got a lot of work done; the house was clean. I wanted sex, lots of it.

Then it was as if someone lit Halloween sparklers in my nervous system. Everything got jangly. I was out of sorts, moody. Sudden inexplicable bursts of anger. I picked fights with everyone. Then the pain. I would lie in bed, my knees drawn up to my chest. Only codeine would take the sharpest edges off the cramping, leaving me dopey with a dull ache in my belly.

Often, I dreamt of water. Playing in the waves at the seaside, the waves got bigger and bigger, I was terrified of drowning. I was in the basement of an old house, there was a leak, water was getting in, the basement was flooding. I was in a canoe, alone, in the middle of a lake, resting my paddle. The sky opened up and sheets of rain came teeming down, filling the frail boat.

Then, at last, the blood. A release, a pleasurable, sensual sensation. Blood is to the body as poetry is to language. It is concentrated, as a poem concentrates language; my very psyche, it seemed, bleeding down and out between my legs. Concentration—and consecration.

Then came a time, which lasted about three years, when my nervous system was constantly on high alert. I couldn't sleep, had frequent blinding headaches, and heat regularly flushed my whole body, always at the most inopportune times, in the middle of a meeting full of men for example. Waking me up every few hours, on the nights when I did manage to sleep. I was cranky and irritable all the time.

I was consumed with remorse and regret. I relived every mistake, every unkind thing I ever said or did. I regretted my life. I ardently wished that I had had four children (when I barely managed to white knuckle my way through raising one). Why had I sacrificed my child to my so-called art? What did it matter that I tossed a few mudpies against my own mortality, when I could have achieved immortality through my progeny? I lay in bed at night, imagining them, two boys and two girls, what they would be like, what names I would give them. I wept with the futility of it all. I knew, for the first time, in my very bones, the inexorable, inevitable cruelty of the forced march of time.

My dreams of water became fiercer, more frightening. Floods and hurricanes. Tidal waves. But slowly, slowly, I began to swim. Stroke after stroke, my body calmed, my rapid, erratic breathing became more rhythmic, in pace with my arms and legs, swimming steadily.

One day, I reach the far shore of the lake of remorse. It is dusk, the golden late evening light of an August night in the north. I climb out, wet and glistening. I walk out onto a meadow. There are thousands and thousands of wildflowers. I am walking, a little stooped, I've lost an inch or two. I am walking. Some of my joints ache some of the time, others ache at other times, sometimes all of my joints ache at the same time. The wildflowers lift up their petalled heads in tiny acts of worship. I am walking, walking. My breasts, which have given me and my lovers so much pleasure, and which once sustained a human life, have descended a few inches too.

Walking, I see a woman standing before me, her arms outstretched. I walk into her embrace. Hello, old age, I say. Hello, freedom.

GOING FOR THE GOLD

Until middle age I loved to ice skate. I retained from childhood the ability to skim across the ice, the feeling of speed, the freedom from the constraints of gravity. But severe arthritis in my right knee put a stop to skating, and occasioned years of pain and, finally, surgery and a long slow recovery. I haven't skated for thirty years now. But I never stopped watching figure skating competitions, and I believe that had I time for more than this lifetime, I could be a champion choreographer. I often fall asleep at night fantasizing how I would choreograph singles, doubles, and group figure skating acts.

I can't bend down very low, and now my left knee bothers me some. My balance is still poor since the knee surgery. Nevertheless, I realized that I could probably, even in my seventies, go skating again. A friend loaned me her skates, and off I went to the Thornhill arena Sunday public free skate.

The first sign that all was not as it once was: I couldn't get the damn skates on. Somehow, in the intervening years, my feet had become so much further away from the rest of me. But with quite a lot of help from Frank, who generously came and watched me, I eventually wrangled them on and laced them up. I managed to hobble around the arena, clinging to the boards, walking more than skating. Various people I passed, who were watching their young children from the wings, gave me their thumbs up and applauded when I made it all way around the rink. (Even the ones as young as four were doing better than me.) As Samuel Johnson said of women preachers, it's like dogs standing on their hind feet. Not that they do it well, but that they do it at all.

A woman came up to me and introduced herself as Michelle. "We have beginner adult classes every Saturday night at 9," she said. "Why don't you join us?"

I bought second-hand skates, knee pads, elbow pads, wrist pads and a helmet. I started attending, feeling nauseous with fear an hour or two beforehand, needing Frank to help me put on my skates, my pads, and my helmet. And to provide moral support. Each session they give me a minder (perhaps afraid of lawsuits should I injure myself)—usually a fifteen- or sixteen-year-old boy or girl. These youngsters are lovely and patient teachers. I alternate clinging to the boards or to their outstretched hands. Week by week I am making incremental progress. When I finally skated all by myself across the width of the rink, not holding on to my minder, I was elated, so exhilarated I couldn't sleep.

One night I arrived at the rink to find out that the class was cancelled, but that a young woman named Melanie would still skate with me. Melanie was the perfect teacher, giving me slightly more challenging ice tasks, one after the other. "Take my hand, we're going to skate around the whole rink. Now stand at the boards, and push your skates out, scrape them out to the sides. This is how you stop. Now skate two feet away from the boards, skate up to them, and push your skates out. There, you've just learned how to stop!" I knew if I could skate once a week with Melanie my progress would soar.

Around this time, I heard about and watched a documentary about five women in Kelowna, all seniors, who competed in the International Skating Union's 2018 competition in Oberstdorf, Germany. Apparently, these competitions are in ten-year increments, ages fifty to fifty-nine, sixty to sixty-nine, seventy to seventy-nine, and eighty and above.

I'm now seventy-five. The pandemic has put a pause in my plans to figure skate again. But when the lessons resume, I still intend to enter the competition in the over-eighty category. There won't be much competition. First, I'll be just eighty, so I'll have the clear advantage of being among the youngest skaters. Also, many, if not most, octogenarian skaters will be dead, or certainly no longer skating, by then.

I figure I have five years to own the podium.

END NOTES

This collection of essays is an archaeology of the self. Sifting through the midden of consciousness, examining potsherds, shells, a broken piece of mirror.

My sister once told me, when I was a child and she was a teenager, that it was the mark of a stupid man to put salt on his food before he tasted it. (This was when all the pronouns were male.) I mention this because I think of it whenever I use salt, which is frequently. My partner looks at every meal I put in front of him, and says, my this looks delicious, before liberally sprinkling it with salt and robustly grinding pepper all over it. But why this seemingly inconsequential memory, over all the many other things she told me, as a big sister, with such authority? Why did this one stick?

It's like gifts. Whenever I use, or even look at, a present that someone gave me, no matter how long ago, I still see that person, still remember that relationship. Each object is mnemonic, carries the aura, the numinosity of the person who gave it to me. Even if it's a fridge magnet, or a dish towel. My friend Carol gave me a woven taupe dish towel I enjoy using. We've been friends for over fifty years, only one of them spent in the same city. We've maintained contact with letters, phone calls and presents, and I can see the marble paperweight she gave me from where I sit at this computer. I remember the red, purple, and white bolero I crocheted for her in the sixties, when I survived endless political meetings with endless needlework.

Where is the past? It can't be seen or touched, but it can be felt.

One morning recently I picked up the phone to hear the voice of Henry, my first lover and first husband, who I've written about twice in this collection. His wife saw "Ginger Cookies," the piece in *The Grapevine*, the local Annapolis Valley newspaper, about living with him in Berwick, Nova Scotia, in the 1960s. He said it brought back so many memories for him. We had a very sweet talk. He's eighty-five now, still running his blueberry and cranberry farms in the Valley. I noticed he was speaking rather slowly, and attributed it to age, but no, he'd had a stroke four years ago. My father gave him his start in business, and under his tutelage he became extremely successful, eventually, like my father, making what's euphemistically called a bundle on the stock market. The last time I'd heard from him was after my father died, in 2006, when he offered to give me some money, quite a lot of money, in honour of my father. I said I didn't really need anything, and that perhaps he should give it to charity. He very decidedly put the kibosh on that idea. Talk to your brother, he said, ask him what he thinks. I called my brother. "Take the fucking money!" became an oft quoted phrase in my life. I thanked Henry again during this more recent conversation and mentioned some of the trips his gift had paid for.

"Well," he said, "I wanted to do something for you, because you're still a part of me."

"Likewise," I said.

For days after this call I wandered around with that whole period of my life in the forefront of my consciousness. The past *was* the present. So clear, so immediate, so bittersweet. I fell in love with Henry when I was sixteen, and I fell out of love with him when I was twenty-two. We were certainly not meant to spend our lives together. We each had a destiny to fulfill, and we did. But how his hair looked, the way he walked, the sound of his voice, are as real to me in my inner senses now as they were in life.

My memories are mine and mine alone. Henry has a different rendition of those years; I'm not sure Carol even remembers that hand-made vest I made for her, the colours chosen so carefully to go with her dark hair and dark eyes and very pale skin. But I can see it, I can remember the feel of the wool being guided by my fingers, as the crochet hook went in and out, and the flower shapes accumulated until there were enough to make something to wear. Enough to make this memory.

My sister had, and still has, a vast store of memorized nursery rhymes, quotations, and song lyrics. I have a few myself:

> I do not love thee Doctor Fell
> The reason why I cannot tell
> But this I know and know it well,
> I do not love thee Doctor Fell.

This scrap of doggerel swims up into my mind. Why remember it? It's of no consequence to anything I can think of. Why this one? It's a mystery.

One day, sweeping the kitchen floor, the phrase "Two tears for Communism" jumped into my mind. I recognized it as a gloss on a collection of essays by E.M. Forster called *Two Cheers for Democracy*. I grieved for the death, not of the Soviet Union and the Soviet bloc countries, but of the great utopian vision held by artists, poets, and revolutionaries at the turn of the last century, a vision that inspired so much, and led to so much blood. What I didn't realize, as I swept, was that this phrase would generate two years of art-making.

Where do ideas come from, asks Chairman Mao on a popular poster from the sixties. Do they come from the sky? No, they come from social practice.

Where do my ideas come from? Not from research, not from conscious effort, not even from inspiration. I sit down to write, and something transpires, something manifests itself. I only ever come back to this word: a mystery.

I turn to my trusty old friend, the good Rabbi Ernest Klein and his *Etymological Dictionary of the English Language*, a tome I've had by my side over the years for many and varied purposes.

"Mystery", from Middle English, from Latin and from
Greek: sacred rites; one initiated into the mysteries; one
whose eyes are closed; to shut or close the lips or eyes; a
muttering sound made with the lips; a groan."

What is the relationship between inspiration, memory, mystery?

Rabbi Klein was a Holocaust survivor who believed that etymol-
ogy was the road to world peace. If people understood that the roots
of all words come from the same place, some mystic origin point, he
believed we would be more tolerant, and have more compassion for
one another. I've often wondered what that *ur*-word might be, the
single word from which all language is generated. "Void," perhaps,
or "Jehovah," or "Sh'ma," meaning "hear," the great prayer said in
every Jewish service: *Sh'ma Yisrael Adonai Eloheinu Adonai Ehad*,
"Hear O Israel, the Lord thy God, the Lord thy God is one." Or
maybe it's just a sound, *Om*, or not even a sound. A breath.

Perhaps it's an image. Perhaps underlying the mystery, inspiration, memory, consciousness itself, is a small white feather dancing
on a gust of wind.

As I write this I'm subsumed with a great longing, an ache. I'm
not sure for what, exactly. My past self, the past itself? I wouldn't be
twenty again, or forty, or even sixty, for any price. Old age is so much
more peaceful, more tranquil, than anything that went before. The
only thing we have to contend with is grief, and that gets better with
practice; and God knows, the older we get, the more practice we get.

The question isn't just: What are we doing here? The question is
also: Why do we have to go? This yearning is also for the ones I
loved, both those who are still with us yet I no longer see, and those
I can't, at least in this lifetime, ever see again. One of the saddest
stories I ever heard was told me by my friend Mary Ellen, who'd lost
her mother when she was fourteen. She said the hardest part of losing her was losing, as Mary Ellen entered her mid-sixties, the memories of her.

What if one day, everyone with whom we've shared some part of
our past, of our lives, is no longer here, if our memories echo and
re-echo through long, empty corridors? Until they too, grow silent.

ACKNOWLEDGEMENTS

This book, like my life, is in many ways the result of conversations —the talks I've had over the years with close friends, some lasting for decades. Conversations about life, art, politics, spirituality, (and let's not forget gossip). Equal parts profound and hilarious. I am deeply grateful to the following friends for being unwitting collaborators in the writing of this book: Mary Ellen Belfiore, Sarah Bugeja, Linda Duvall, Melanie Fernandez, Mary Finlay, Carol Hay, Ken Klonsky, Joss Maclennan, John Miller, m. nourbeSe philip, Clare Samuel, Kelly Scott, Kathleen Whelan, Megan Williams.

And deep gratitude to those voices I can no longer hear: Brian Shein, Terry McAuliffe, Kent Biggar, Dayne Ogilvie, Nena Hardie, Diana Meredith, John McLean, Carol Morrell.

Thank you to David Hayes and Lorri Neilsen Glenn, my mentors at the University of Kings College MFA in Creative Nonfiction; the members of the Marguaretta Street Writing Group in Toronto; the Adrift Collective in Vancouver; and the Kings Gang of Five Writing Group in cyberspace.

And thanks also to Michael Mirolla and the team at Guernica Editions.

ABOUT THE AUTHOR

Robin Pacific is a single malt drinking Anglican socialist. She was born in Vancouver, did a BA in Halifax, and an MA and PhD in Toronto. She subsequently received a Masters in Theological Studies at Regis College in the University of Toronto School of Divinity and an MFA in Creative Nonfiction at the University of Kings College in Halifax. She always believed she would become a writer, but took a twenty-five year detour to work as a visual artist. Her art practice encompasses drawing, painting, video, performance, computer art, installations, and large community-based collaborative projects. She was a founder of Art Starts, a community art centre which is still thriving and works with professional and nonprofessional artists from underserved neighbourhoods. Robin has always been passionate about the trifecta of art, spirituality, and social justice. For ten years she has had a part time practice as a Spiritual Director. She continues to make art, write, and do spiritual counselling in Toronto. This is her first book. Her artist's website is www.robinpacific.ca, and her writer's site is www.robinpacificwriter.com.